IMPERIALISTIC RELIGION

AND

THE RELIGION OF DEMOCRACY

IMPERIALISTIC RELIGION

AND THE

RELIGION OF DEMOCRACY

A STUDY IN SOCIAL PSYCHOLOGY

BY

WILLIAM ADAMS BROWN, Ph.D., D.D.

AUTHOR OF
"CHRISTIAN THEOLOGY IN OUTLINE" "THE CHURCH IN AMERICA"
ETC.

NEW YORK
CHARLES SCRIBNER'S SONS
1923

MADE AND PRINTED IN GREAT BRITAIN BY MORRISON AND GIBB LTD. EDINBURGH

TO

CHRISTIANS WHO DIFFER

PREFACE

THE subject to which the following pages are devoted has occupied my thoughts for many years. In these days when there is so much talk of unity, it is more than ever necessary that we should give time to the study of differences. Especially is it important that we should learn to distinguish between the differences which are due to temporary or removable causes, and those which are rooted in human nature, or, what comes to much the same thing, are the result of conditions in the environment which are likely to recur from age to age.

A notable contribution to the study of these more deep-seated differences was made by Professor William James in his well-known book on *The Varieties of the Religious Experience.* The present inquiry takes up the discussion where Professor James leaves off. It deals with the attitude of religious people to society and the institutions it creates—a subject which James expressly excluded from his own consideration. But in spite of this difference of immediate objective, the underlying interest is the same. Like Professor James, I shall study varieties of the religious experience, in the hope of clarifying our understanding of the nature of religion.

So far as I am aware, the particular classification here suggested has not been used in the precise form in which I use it by any previous writer. If I am in error in this I shall be glad to be corrected. In any case, it is evident that a generalization of so sweeping a character will need to be rigorously tested before it can be accepted. I could have wished to make my own test more thorough and detailed than has been possible in the time hitherto at my disposal. But it has seemed to me that the advantages of early criticism by others interested in the subject would more than outweigh the disadvantages necessarily connected with the presentation of so important a thesis in a condensed form, and without the critical apparatus by which the scholar is accustomed to fortify his conclusions.

Of the inadequacy of the last chapter I am fully conscious. The study of religious differences makes us more than ever aware of our need of some principle of unity, and the questions where such a principle is to be found and how it is to be recognized deserve a more thoroughgoing treatment than I have been able to give them in this book. Men of every type of religious

experience are forced sooner or later to come
to terms with historic religion. The democrat
especially, with his forward look and his catholic
sympathies, needs a firm grounding for his faith
in history so that he may feel his unity with men
of other ages and of other types. No one has a
more vital interest than the democrat in the great
personality from whom Christianity takes its
name, or in the unique literature which preserves
his life-story and mediates his present spirit.
None needs a clearer appreciation of the fact that
the God of this age is the God of all the ages, and
that, in this changing world, progress, so far from
being inconsistent with permanence, is the way in
which we make our own the eternal values.

The substance of the following pages was delivered as the Martha Upton Lectures in Religion
for 1922, at Manchester College, Oxford, under the
title " Three Great Religions." Parts of Chapters
I., III., IV., and V. were delivered at King's
College of the University of London, in the fall of
the same year, under the title " The Religion of
Democracy." The main thesis to which the work
is devoted was presented to the Aristotelian
Society of London in January 1923, in a
paper entitled " The Problem of Classification in
Religion."

I wish to express my thanks to the Faculty of
Manchester College ; to the Divinity Faculty

of the University of London ; and to the authorities
of King's College for the opportunity their in-
vitations have afforded me to clarify my own
thinking ; and to the audiences whose sympathetic following of the lectures during their
delivery has encouraged me to hope that the line
of thought they present may prove of interest
to a wider public.

WILLIAM ADAMS BROWN.

New York City,
  September 1923.

CONTENTS

CHAPTER I

THE PROBLEM OF VARIATION IN RELIGION

CHAPTER II

RELIGION AS PERSONAL EXPERIENCE AND AS HISTORIC PROCESS

CHAPTER III

IMPERIALISTIC RELIGION: ITS NATURE
AND VARIETIES

CHAPTER IV

THE INDIVIDUALISTIC PROTEST AGAINST IMPERIALISM

CHAPTER V

DEMOCRATIC RELIGION

CHAPTER I

THE PROBLEM OF VARIATION IN RELIGION

1. *Need of a New Study of Religious Types*

THE problem which we are to consider in the pages that follow is one of the oldest, one of the most interesting, and one of the most difficult in the study of religion. It is the problem of the origin and of the significance of differing religious types. If religion be the most important thing in human life, as multitudes of men have believed, how comes it that we differ so widely as to what religion *is*? If there is really a God who reveals Himself to man, why does He not make His presence known in ways which cannot be misinterpreted? Why are men still at variance in their view of what God has revealed and what He wants from His worshippers?

I am going to propose a new answer to this question. At least I am going to suggest a new angle from which some of the old answers may be approached. But before I state what that angle is and explain my reasons for making it my point of departure, it may be of interest if I

take a moment or two to explain how I have
been led to make this inquiry.

In the course of my work as a teacher it has
been my duty for many years to study religious
experience, under the heads by which it is described in the familiar text-books in theology—
such terms as natural and revealed, Catholic and
Protestant, Traditionalist and Modernist, mystical
and ethical religion. But the historic situations
which I have been called upon to analyse have
proved too complicated to be treated in this way.
Too many facts remained unaccounted for. Too
many were inconsistent with the explanations
which were given of them. I was forced to
realize that from the point of view of scientific
theory, our existing classifications needed to be
restudied.

Then the war came, and for the moment
practice crowded out theory. Every man's
attention was turned to the needs of the critical
moment. It fell to my lot during the years of
the war, and the scarcely less trying years that
have succeeded it, to try to help many different
kinds of Christians to do work together. The
merely theoretical interest which I had hitherto
had in the problem of classification in religion
was now reinforced by motives of the most
practical kind. But my new experience led me
to the old conclusion. The names by which
men called themselves did not always correspond
to what they really were. The social groupings
which divided them as Catholic and Protestant,

Presbyterian and Episcopalian, Baptist and Unitarian, by no means always expressed the trend of their dominant interests and sympathies. You could not tell beforehand how a man called an Episcopalian would feel or how he would act. And the same was true of each of the other sectarian and denominational names.

Yet we were constantly acting as if we could. We often judged men, not by what they were, but by what, according to their party name, they ought to be. And this habit gave rise to manifold misunderstandings and bitternesses. Many of these were wholly needless ; yet they shaped party policy, and led to the forming of plans which, in the nature of the case, could not be carried out. For practical reasons, therefore, as well as in the interest of scientific accuracy, a new study of religious types seemed urgently called for.

The need of such a study was again vividly brought home to me at a meeting which I attended in Copenhagen during the summer of 1922. It had been called by the World Alliance for International Friendship through the Churches to consider the existing international situation, and to see what could be done about uniting the Churches in some practicable programme on behalf of world peace. But at the very outset we were confronted by the fact of difference. Not only was there no international organization through which the Churches of different countries could function effectively, but the religious forces of each country were divided. The

English Churches were separated by the wide gap
between the Establishment and Nonconformity,
and the Free Churches differed among themselves.
The denominationalism of American Christianity
has long been a byword. Each Continental
Church faced in its own way the fact of division.
Nor was there division simply in the sphere of
outward organization and polity. There was
lack of unity on fundamental theoretical questions. There was no agreement, for example,
on such a question as this : Has the Church any
responsibility, independently of the State, for
determining standards of social and political
action, or should it confine itself to the cultivation of the purely personal religious life ? In
theory we came together as Christians. In
theory we professed to be adherents of one
religion and worshippers of one God. But in
practice we had not yet found it possible to
work together in any united and effective way.

Nor was this the whole story. One great
division of Christendom was conspicuous by its
absence. A leading Archbishop of the Greek
Church attended the meeting at Copenhagen,
but no Roman Catholic was present. This was
not due to inadvertence. Representatives of
the Roman Church had been privately sounded
as to the possibility of their attendance. It was
not due to any lack of interest in the subject to
be discussed. Roman Catholics are just as much
concerned to secure world peace as Anglicans
or Presbyterians. It was due to a deep-seated

difference of religious conviction. This difference was so fundamental that the representatives of a great Church were unwilling to sit around the same table, in discussion with their fellow-Christians, under conditions which might seem to imply equality between them.

Obviously this is a fact of outstanding importance. It raises a very searching question. When for centuries religious men have been unwilling to meet face to face in the common practice of the rites of their religion, have we any right to regard them as belonging to the same religion ? Eminent scholars have answered this question in the negative.

Thus Tiele, in his *Introduction to the Study of Religion*,[1] denies that we have any right to speak of Christianity as one religion. " In Christianity as in Buddhism," he tells us, " we have to do, not with a single religion, but with a family of religions, which to be sure in their origin and in certain general principles are one ; but for the rest are at most points widely separated and even hostile, one to the other, a group or family of religions, like the Aryan or Semitic. These groups, which we call the Christian and Buddhist religions, are differentiated from other groups in that they are still conscious of a common origin and relative spiritual relationship, simply because their origin has fallen in historic times, while that of the older groups belongs to the prehistoric period."

[1] *Einleitung in die Religionswissenschaft*, Eng. trans., p. 124.

Sharply as this view contradicts conventional opinion, there is much to be said in its favour. When we contrast the different forms of historic Christianity with one another, it seems impossible to bring them all under a single name. What is there in common between the contemplative religion of the Russian mystic and the militant faith of an ultramontane Roman Catholic ? What community of feeling can there be between the high Anglican, devoted to liturgy and sacrament, and the free and unconventional evangelical ? What a shudder the very name Unitarian calls forth in some Christians who have been taught to regard the Trinity as the *articulus stantis aut cadentis ecclesiæ* !

The extent and wide diversity of these variations within Christianity have been described by Dr. McGiffert in an impressive passage in the *Hibbert Journal* [1] as follows :

" From the beginning, one of the extraordinary things about Christianity has been its great variety. To the Apostle Paul, to Ignatius of Antioch, and to thousands of believers since, a religion of redemption, releasing men from the trammels of the world and sin and death, and giving them the power of an endless life. To Justin Martyr, to Pelagius, to Socinus, a revelation of God's will which we have abundant ability to obey if we but choose, and obeying which we reap the fitting reward. To Clement of Alexandria, to Scotus Erigena, to Frederick William Hegel, to speculative thinkers of every age, a

[1] "Christianity in the Light of its History," July 1913, p. 717 seq.

philosophy of the universe, explaining the whence and the whither, the beginning and the end of all things. To the schoolmen, both Catholic and Protestant, the acceptance of a series of propositions, supposed to contain final and absolute truth touching God and man and the universe. To St. Bernard and Fénelon and William Law, to the mystics of all generations, the transcendence of human limitations in oneness with the divine. To St. Francis of Assisi and Thomas à Kempis, and many a lovely spirit of our own and other days, the imitation of Christ in His life of poverty, humility, and love. To Cyprian and Augustine and countless Catholics, the one holy, apostolic Church, an ark of salvation, alone providing escape from eternal punishment. To Hildebrand and Innocent, as to modern ultramontanists in general, the papal hierarchy, ruler of the nations of the earth. To Benedict of Nursia, to Boniface the Saxon Apostle, to not a few missionaries of these latter days, a great civilizing agency, raising whole peoples from ignorance and savagery to culture and humaneness. To the rationalist of the eighteenth century, the religion of nature, always one and unchanging, the worship of God and the pursuit of virtue. To a growing multitude of Christians of our own day, humanitarianism, the service of one's fellows in the spirit of Jesus Christ."

"These," Dr. McGiffert goes on to say, "were not simply different phases of the same faith; these were often altogether different faiths. They were not the mere development of an original principle, the life and work and teaching of Jesus of Nazareth : they were many

of them fresh creations. Their secret lay in the
fact that Christianity has always been the vital
faith of individuals, and not merely a public or
national cult. Out of varied human experiences,
determined by character, by temperament, by
education, by example, the new ways of looking
at things arose. Often forces entirely alien to
Christianity had their part in producing them,
and few of them would have been recognized by
Jesus Himself as an interpretation of His own
faith or of His own ideals.''

The question which we are raising is not,
then, subsidiary or unimportant : it touches the
very heart and inner shrine of religion. It is not
only interesting scientifically as a problem for
the mind. It is not only important practically,
for our guidance in co-operative endeavour. It
brings us face to face with the central problem
of all religion, the problem of Revelation. If,
as religion assumes, God has revealed Himself in
a permanent and authoritative way, how do we
reconcile this fact of revelation with the dis-
crepancies in existing religion ? In the conflict of
rival interpretations, how can we tell where the
truth lies ? Our study may not furnish us with
a complete answer to this question. But it may
remove some present difficulties in the way of
such an answer.

2. *The Phenomena needing Explanation*

At the risk of going over familiar ground, it
may be helpful to remind ourselves of some

of the present outstanding religious differences. First of all there is the difference between those imposing social complexes which we call the historic religions—the rival faiths which divide between them the allegiance of most of mankind, and which are represented on the missionary maps in bold contrasts of white, yellow, green, and black. In contrast to one another, each of these faiths represents a certain principle of unity. The Christian, the Mohammedan, and the Buddhist are each conscious of an ancestry, of traditions and of a literature, which bind them to their co-religionists and separate them from the members of rival groups. Each group has its Bible, which its members read. Each group has its founder, whom all its members revere. The relation of these historic unities to the internal differences which separate members of the same group presents difficulties —difficulties which we will discuss later on— but the unities cannot be denied.

Next there are the differences which appear within the different religions. These differences are of two kinds—differences of organization and differences of conviction. That singular phenomenon in Protestantism which we call the denomination is a religious organization which has all the marks of a complete Church, and yet which recognizes other similar Churches within the same religion. Catholicism has its religious orders and societies that cut across the existing diocesan organization, and make room within the

one inclusive Catholic Church, for the initiative
and rivalry which in Protestantism are expressed
through independent Churches. In the United
States, where denominationalism has been carried
farthest, the Census of 1916 registers nearly two
hundred self-governing and practically independent bodies. While many of these are so
small as to be negligible, there are more than
fifty that number over fifty thousand, and of
families that approach or surpass the million
there are eight.

To differences of organization must be added
differences of conviction ; and the two by no
means always correspond. As the peoples of the
different nations and States are divided into
parties, so all these different Churches and
denominations are divided into schools. There
are High Churchmen and Low Churchmen,
Broad Churchmen and Evangelicals, Modernists
and Traditionalists, Sacramentarians [1] and those
who have no use for institutional religion. The
views of each of these groups are in process of
constant modification. As soon as the existing
forms prove inadequate some new school arises
or some new party is formed.

Finally we have the differences which are due
to variation in the individual religious experience.
In religion, as in other phases of man's life,
temperament is an influential factor. The

----

[1] I use the word here in the most general sense, to designate
the type of religion in which the sacrament rather than the
sermon is made central in public worship.

familiar contrasts between the rationalist and the mystic, the individualist and the churchman, the soul which bows unquestioningly before external authority, and the free and inquiring spirit :—these differences make themselves perenially felt in religious history, and affect the larger social groupings, in interesting and often perplexing ways.

One may react to these familiar differences in different ways. One may ignore their existence. I suspect this attitude is much more common than we often realize. I do not mean, of course, that we are not aware that there are other forms of religion than our own, but that these do not enter in any real way into our daily life. They do not interest us. We do not feel any responsibility for understanding them. If we think of them at all, it is as of inadequate and outgrown forms with which we have no concern. Religion for most of us means—for all practical purposes —our own religion.

To one brought up in this way, the discovery of other religions is a moving experience. I vividly remember when I first began to realize that the Greek Church is alive—an institution through which millions of fellow-Christians worship God to-day—and is not merely the relic of a past stage in the history of the Christian religion. It was on a first visit to Russia. Driving in Moscow we passed a street-icon and our driver paused an instant to cross himself devoutly. I caught the look in his eyes as he fixed them upon the picture, and from that moment I was able to think of Greek Christianity as a living thing.

3. *The View which explains Religious Differences as due to the Contrast between True and False Religion*

The best known, as it is the oldest, of the theoretical explanations of the existing differences is that which attempts to account for them by their origin. According to this view religions differ as true or false. Some religions are human inventions, others owe their origin to divine revelation. Only the latter can promise the enlightenment and help man needs. Thus Christianity, as the revealed religion, differs from all merely natural or ethnic faiths, because while Christianity is based upon a definite and authoritative revelation of God, they are so many attempts of human reason to solve for itself a problem, which without supernatural help is in its very nature insoluble.

The contrast between true and false religion is not confined to Christianity. All the greater historic religions assume the possession of an infallible divine revelation, and contrast their own faith as true with that of their rivals as false. Each of the great religions has its Bible and its Church, its priesthood and its temples, and each professes to give certainty and assurance to its worshippers. The existence of false religions is accounted for in different ways, either as an unconscious witness to the existence of a true revelation by those who do not possess it, or as a manifestation of the pride and wickedness of the perverted human heart. But all agree that their own religion possesses unchanging truth. It alone has persisted unaltered through the centuries.

A monk of the convent of Alexander Nevsky in Petrograd once told me the story of his conversion from Lutheranism to the orthodox faith. He had investigated all the forms of historic Christianity which were known to him, Protestant and Catholic alike, and had come to rest at last in the bosom of the Greek Church. He had written out the story of his quest in a little volume entitled *How I found the True Church*, a sort of Russian *Apologia pro Vitâ Suâ*. The motives which had led him to his final decision were in the last analysis two: his æsthetic satisfaction with the worship of the Orthodox Church, and the fact that it alone of all existing forms of Christianity had preserved the primitive deposit of faith absolutely unchanged.

The theory of religion which explains the existing differences by their departure from a single unchanging revelation requires a similar explanation of the differences within the different religions. These also are to be brought under the categories of true and false. If God has given a single authoritative revelation, there can be no room for difference or dispute as to what He has

said. There must be one standard to which all
conform. That which agrees with it is true.
That which differs from it must be false. The
name given to false manifestations within a true
religion is heresy. We all know how great a rôle
this conception has played—not only in Christianity, but in the other great religions. I have
in my library a book by a Mohammedan scholar
on the seventy-three sects of Islam. With great
patience and learning he describes the differences
in the teaching and practices of these rival sects.
The importance of his results becomes evident
when he reminds his reader that of all seventy-
three ways, only one offers him any hope of
reaching Paradise.[1]

4. *The View which regards them as Steps in the
   Development of a Single All - embracing
   Religion*

Without minimizing the distinction between
the true and the false in religion, or overlooking
the importance of the question whether God has,
in fact, revealed Himself, and by what mark this

---

[1] An alternative use of the distinction between true and
false may be referred to in passing. The Deists, as is well
known, identified true religion with the religion of nature which
is everywhere and always the same, and regarded the claim of
the historic religions to possess an additional supernatural
revelation as false. From their point of view, as truly as that
of the orthodox theologians they opposed, there could be only
one true religion—namely, their own—and the differences which
emerge in history, and which constitute our present problem,
were all alike explained as forms of superstition.

revelation is to be recognized, I think it can be said without fear of misunderstanding that the attitude of undiscriminating condemnation of all religions but one's own has proved untenable. Face to face with the concrete facts of existing religion, the most convinced traditionalists have not been able to deny that the ethnic faiths contain some measure of truth. They have explained its presence in different ways. Some have accounted for it as the corruption of an original divine revelation which, in spite of all imperfection, still retains marks of a divine origin. Others have interpreted it as due to human aspiration—the strivings of the soul after God divinely implanted in man's nature. Most frequently they have seen in it a real though lower stage of divine revelation, meant to prepare the way for the fuller revelation to come. Even on this theory some other principle of classification is obviously needed ; some alternative, or, at least, some supplementary explanation of existing difference. Such an explanation has been found by many scholars in the principle of development. According to this view the differences between existing forms of religion are due to the different place which they hold in the unfolding of religion as a whole. They differ, not as true and false, but as more or less true.

The idea of development, to be sure, carries with it no necessary connotation of progress. As used by biologists to explain the origin of species it is simply the story of the emergence

of more complex forms of organization. But this
purely scientific conception has been paralleled
by a movement in philosophy in which the
conception of development has been applied to
man's moral and religious history. Herder and
Lessing were leaders in this movement ; Herder
in his epoch-making work, *Ideen zur Geschichte
der Menschheit*,[1] Lessing in his more popular
treatise on the *Education of the Human Race*.[2]

This conception has had its reflex influence
upon the study of religion. The different religions have come to be regarded as parts of one
all-embracing religion, as steps through which
the human spirit is ascending in its quest of God.
The most famous representative of this new
method of dealing with the problem of variation
in religion, and its most original interpreter, was
Hegel. Hegel explained the entire phenomena
of religious history as steps in the unfolding of
a single all-inclusive religion—a process through
which, by slow degrees, proceeding from the less
to the more perfect in an ever-ascending series,
the truth, which had been implicit in religion
from the first, was made explicit in definite beliefs,
precepts, and practices.[3]

The Hegelian method, as is well known, had
a great vogue in its day. It was applied not
only to the explanation of the differences between
the historic religions, but of the inner divisions

---

[1] 1784–1791.　　　　　　　[2] 1780.

[3] On the Hegelian philosophy of religion, cf. W. Adams
Brown, *The Essence of Christianity*, New York, 1902, p. 186 seq.

within each. Baur and his school applied it to the interpretation of Christian doctrine, and regarded Catholicism and Protestantism as successive steps in the unfolding of the Christian religion. Students of comparative religion grouped the existing religions in an ascending series according to some principle of immanent development. The methods followed differed widely in detail. Sometimes departure was taken from the idea of God, and we have the series, henotheism, polytheism, monotheism, pantheism. Sometimes the end sought in religion was the determining principle, and we have the distinction between natural religion, which is concerned with happiness and prosperity, and ethical religion, which makes character the goal. The religion of this world was contrasted with other-worldly religion, the religion of self-fulfilment with that of redemption. Still again, attention was directed to the social aspects of religion, and we have religions classified as tribal, national, or universal, according to the range of their social consciousness. But in each case the individual religion was conceived as part of a larger religious development, a stage through which the possibilities of religion as a whole were unfolded.

It is not difficult to point out the limitations of this method. They can all be summed up in a single sentence. The classifications given do not correspond to the facts. The varieties in the existing religions are too great to make possible their tabulation as parts of a single consistent logical

2

scheme. Each religion, and to a very considerable extent, each lesser unit within each religion, is a complex in which many of the contrasted types are found. Granting that the distinctions made are correct as far as they go, and I for one believe that every one of them points to a real difference of which we ought to take account, the attempt to identify them with existing historic religions is hopeless from the start. The only way to arrange religious phenomena so as to give a truthful account of religion as it really is, is first of all to find some classification which is independent of the complex groups we call the historic religions. Only when we have learned to understand religion as an experience of living men facing a changing environment can we hope to understand the different forms which it has assumed in the course of its historic development. In a word, we must find our principle of classification in psychology.

5. *Psychological Classifications, Individualistic and Social*

Much patient effort has been expended in the attempt to find such a classification, and many learned books have been written. The solutions proposed are of various kinds, but they agree in this, that we can understand the existing differences in religious types only if we regard them as proceeding from inherent differences in human nature, and therefore likely to recur within all religions as long as man remains what he is.[1] I believe that this view of the matter is substantially correct, and the classification which I shall suggest follows this line. It is psychological, in that it takes its departure from the attitude of religious people. But it differs from many of the more familiar psychological classifications in that it finds its determining principle in man's attitude towards organized society.

In suggesting man's attitude towards society as a principle of religious classification, I am far from claiming complete originality. The use of social categories to explain religious differences is not uncommon. But most of those who have followed this method have taken their departure from some existing historic unit which they wished to interpret. Their primary interest has been historical or theological rather than psychological. They wished to explain the differences between the historic forms of religion, or to gain some clue to the better understanding of their own. Thus Harnack takes his departure from the familiar contrast between Catholic and Protestant, and writes the history of Christianity as the story of the emergence and development of three parallel and competing forms of religion—the Greek, the

---

[1] This does not mean that human nature is something rigid and changeless, but only that different people tend to react to a particular situation in different ways, and that this difference of tendency is a permanent fact, of which, if we are wise, we shall take account.

Roman, and the Protestant.[1] Sabatier distinguishes the religion of authority from the religion
of the Spirit, and finds two main types of the
former, the religion of the Church and the religion
of the Book.[2] Troeltsch also adopts a threefold

[1] Harnack's classification is given in his well-known lectures,
entitled *What is Christianity?* (1900; Eng. trans., 1901). In this
book, Harnack tells the story of the Christian religion as that
of the emergence, and conflict of three parallel and rival forms
of Christianity—Greek Christianity, Roman Christianity, and
Protestantism. These are not, as Baur and the Hegelian school
had maintained, steps in the development of the Christian
religion, but parallel and in many respects inconsistent forms of
religion. Each claims to cover the whole ground. Each is
certain of possessing the complete truth. Each shows the
qualities of churchly as distinct from individual or sectarian
religion. Between them they seem to Harnack to exhaust the
logical possibilities. He sees no room for any other. There
may be changes within each. There may be development and
progress. But this development will give rise to no new form,
important enough to take its place as a fourth member in the
classification. Even the changes produced by modern science
are for the purposes of religious classification negligible. Modern
Protestantism, so often contrasted with the religion of the
Reformation as a distinct type, represents to Harnack no new
form of the Christian religion. It is an inner-Protestant development, interesting and important, but not important enough to
require any structural change, similar to that which divides
Protestantism from its two older sisters of the Christian family.

For a criticism of this classification, cf. my article " Is our
Protestantism still Protestant ? " *Harvard Theological Review*,
Jan. 1908, p. 28 seq.

[2] Sabatier's classification is given in his posthumous work,
The Religions of Authority and the Religion of the Spirit (1904 ;
Eng. trans., New York, 1904). Sabatier finds Harnack's treatment unsatisfactory in two ways. In the first place it separates
types which belong together. In the second place it fails to
distinguish types which should be separated. Harnack distinguishes three parallel forms of historic Christianity—Greek
Catholicism, Roman Catholicism, and Protestantism. But to

classification, but his triad consists of the religion
of the Church, the religion of the sect, and mystical
religion which is purely individualistic.[1]

The classification presently to be suggested
approaches the subject from a different angle.
In all the above classifications, as we have seen,
the historic interest is controlling.   The aim is to

Sabatier Greek and Roman Catholicism, widely as they differ
from one another, are yet both forms of the religion of the Church.
Both attribute final authority to an external organization whose
utterance is identified with the voice of God.   Both contend
that this Church has preserved the deposit of faith unchanged,
and therefore deserves the unquestioning submission of all who
desire salvation.

Under Protestantism, on the other hand, Harnack combines
two types of religion which, according to Sabatier, should be
distinguished.   There is the old dogmatic Protestantism of the
creeds and the systems, which substitutes the Bible for the
Church as the infallible revelation of God, but for the rest requires
for it the same unquestioning submission which the Catholic
asks for the Councils or the Pope.   There is, on the other hand,
modern Protestantism which recognizes the right of the free
spirit to judge for itself, and holds that God is most truly known
when each man decides for himself what is true.   But the same
free spirit is found in Catholicism in the movement we know as
Modernism.   Sabatier, then, would substitute for the threefold
classification of Harnack, a new division, also threefold—namely,
the religion of the Church, the religion of the Book, and the
religion of the Spirit.

[1] For the details of Troeltsch's classification see his imposing
monograph on the social teaching of the Christian Churches
(*Die Soziallehren der christlichen Kirchen und Gruppen*, Tübingen,
1919, pp. 358–426).   He distinguishes three types of historic
religion—the Church type, the sect type, and the mystical type.
The first makes the institution as such the final norm of religion.
The second identifies the truth with the teaching of a school or
party.   The third makes the individual soul the final arbiter
of truth, and the appointed meeting-place of God and man.   In
all these we have to do with parallel competing types, each of
which claims to cover the whole field of the religious experience.

understand the existing differences in Christianity. In the classification we shall propose the psychological interest is dominant. We shall ask in what way does the religious individual react to his social environment, whatever that environment may be. What are the possible attitudes which man may take toward existing social institutions, and how far do we find these differing social attitudes expressing themselves in contrasted types of religious experience? The two inquiries are not unrelated, nor need their results be inconsistent. Indeed it may well prove that the psychological approach will bring to light aspects of the religious experience which might otherwise elude the historian.

The psychological approach to religious problems is not a modern discovery. Schleiermacher used it with remarkable originality and power, and in this he was following older masters, notably the master psychologist of the ancient Church, Augustine. From his Northampton study, Jonathan Edwards made notable contribution to the psychological study of religion in his *Treatise on the Religious Affections* (1746). Such distinctions as that between mystical, rational or dogmatic, and practical religion have long been commonplaces of the systematic theologian. But it is only in comparatively recent times that the professional psychologist has begun to concern himself with religious problems. This new interest has given rise to the discipline of the psychology of religion.

The psychological study of religion has been most actively pursued in the United States.[1] But it was the appearance in 1902 of Professor William James's epoch-making Gifford Lectures on the *Varieties of the Religious Experience*,[2] that did most to focus the attention of the general public upon the problems of personal religion.   The distinction of the author in his chosen field, the international auspices under which his book appeared, together with its charm and originality, combined to attract wide attention to the new theme.   The detailed examination which James gave to the different aspects of the individual religious experience was all to the good, and students of religion, as well as psychologists, have much to learn from his

[1] Professor Starbuck was one of the pioneers of the new study. He tried to throw light on the nature of religion by analysing its contemporary forms, and for this purpose developed the method of the questionnaire.   The questions in which he took the greatest interest were those which were most prominent in the experience of the young men and women whom he studied, such questions as the nature and antecedents of conversion, the nature of prayer and the possibility of its answer, and the like. Others who have followed similar methods are President Stanley Hall of Clark University and Professor Leuba of Bryn Mawr. Professor Ames of the University of Chicago lays stress upon the social aspects of religion, but he does not make the religious man's attitude to society a principle of classification.   A particularly fruitful contribution is that of Professor Stratton (*The Psychology of the Religious Life*, London, 1911), because of the clearness with which he perceives the presence of contrasted emphases in religion, and the thoroughness and originality of his analysis of the most important of them.   The more recent work of Professor Coe and Professor Pratt is familiar to all students of the subject.

[2] London, 1902.

brilliant discussion. It is the more to be re-
gretted that his restriction of his inquiry to the
purely individual aspects of the religious experience should for the moment have diverted
attention from other—and no less important—
factors in the religious life.

Professor James himself was quite alive to
this limitation. The field which he chose for his
investigation was arbitrarily restricted. " What
I propose to study," he said, "is the feelings,
acts, and experiences of individual men in their
solitude, so far as they apprehend themselves to
stand in relation to whatever they may consider
the divine." [1] It is the religion of the solitary
and the saint which James invites us to study ;
the lonely soul in commerce with its God. All
the differences which owe their origin to history
are ignored. Mystical religion is studied, but
ethical religion is touched on but lightly. The
religion which expressed its faith in God by its
love to man receives scant attention.

Within the limits which he has set for himself,
Professor James's work is full of suggestion for
the student of religious types.[2]   His catholic

[1] *Op. cit.* p. 31.

[2] It is true that Professor James himself gives no systematic
classification of religious types even in the field of individualistic
religion.   Indeed it is surprising how little attention psychologists
have hitherto given to this subject.   The appearance of Professor
Jung's important work on *Psychologische Typen* (Zürich, 1921)
has called attention to this neglected field, and it is to be hoped
that in the future it will receive the attention it deserves from
students of the psychology of religion.   Cf. also Tansley, *The
New Psychology*, London, 1920, p. 102 seq.

spirit finds meaning in phases of the religious experience which have hitherto been passed over as negligible, if not condemned as pathological. The mystical experience is analysed in a fresh and stimulating way. The contrast between the conventional religious experience and that of the saint is emphasized, and the significance of the latter pointed out. Especially illuminating is the distinction which Professor James draws between the positive and negative aspects of the religious experience—what he calls the religion of healthy-mindedness and the religion of the sick soul. In the former, normal development is the rule, and there is no acute consciousness of sin ; in the latter—the religion of the twice-born —the soul feels divided against itself, and salvation is sought in some radical change of life.

Professor James will have much to teach us about individualistic religion—one of the three great religious types which we shall study. But even individualistic religion can be conceived rightly only when it is placed in its historic setting, and understood as a protest against existing forms of social religion. The fact is that the distinction which James tries to make between individual and social religion is an impossible one. Man's relation to his God is affected in a hundred ways by his relation to his fellow-men, and no study of religious types can hope to be adequate which does not have constantly in mind the historic forms which we call the religions. This fact is

coming to be recognized to-day.   The psychology
of religion is not proposed as a substitute for the
history of religion, but as a supplement, and the
most recent writers in this field, like Pratt and
Coe, have added to their description of the
phenomena of the individual religious experience
illuminating discussions of the social manifestations of the religious life.[1]

In suggesting a social principle of classification, therefore, we must not be thought to be
abandoning the psychological approach. We are
only applying it in a different context, and to a
larger collection of facts. We need a principle
of classification which shall deal with religion as
a whole, not simply with individual aspects
or manifestations of religion,—a principle which
shall interpret to us the permanent and recurrent
types of *social* religion which not only cut across
the historic religions, but persist within each
historical religion,—a principle, finally, which will
help us to account for existing differences and
to deal with them intelligently.   Such a principle
we may find in man's relation to organized
society.

6. *A Suggested Classification*

There are three possible attitudes which one
may take to existing social institutions. One
may accept them as they are without question,
and yield them willing and loyal allegiance.

[1] Cf. Coe, *Psychology of Religion*, 1916, pp. 107 seq., 246 seq. ;
Pratt, *The Religious Consciousness*, 1920, pp. 68 seq., 255 seq.

One may protest against them as corrupt or negligible, and find in one's own inner life a refuge and compensation. One may believe that society itself is in the process of remaking, and that in the progress towards better things each man and woman may have a part. These three attitudes have their counterparts in religion. There are religious people who are satisfied with the Church as it is, and yield it their willing and hearty allegiance. There are others who regard it as corrupt or negligible and believe that religion is capable of complete description in terms of the relation between God and the individual soul. There are still others who believe that God is using the present Church to train men and women for a better social order, and that it is the privilege of every truly religious person to co-operate in the process.

These three types of religious experience give rise to institutions appropriate to their genius. They are all social forms of religion, wholes, not parts ; religions, not simply types of religious experience.[1] They recur in every age and cut across the great complexes we call the historic religions.   They have as yet no recognized names. For the purpose of this discussion we shall call them *imperialism*, *individualism*, and *democracy*. By imperialism we shall understand a type of religion, the representatives of which believe that they serve God best when they submit

[1] This is true, as we shall see later, even of individualistic religion.   Cf. Chapter IV. p. 118 seq.

to the control of some existing institution whose supremacy in the world they identify with the triumph of God's will. By individualism we shall understand a type of religion whose representatives despair of satisfaction through any existing institution, and find solace in immediate communion between the individual soul and God. By democracy we shall understand a type of religion the representatives of which are convinced that they serve God best when they discover His presence in other persons and unite with them in the progressive realization of the ideal social order which it is God's purpose to establish on earth through the free co-operation of men.

This classification differs from the other social classifications with which I am familiar in two respects. In the first place it groups under the common head of imperialism forms of authoritative religion which other classifications separate. In the second place it distinguishes individualism and democracy as independent types, whereas the best known classifications group them together as religions of freedom in contrast to the religion of authority.[1]

---

[1] Thus Sabatier, as we have seen, distinguishes the religion of the Church and the religion of the Book as religions of authority from the religion of the Spirit. Troeltsch distinguishes the churchly type of religion from the religion of the sect, and both as social forms of religion from mystical religion, which is purely individualistic. Harnack, employing more conventional categories, contrasts Protestantism with the two great forms of Catholicism, that of the Greek Church, in which the emphasis falls upon the past, and Roman Catholicism which possesses

In experience, to be sure, the three types we have distinguished as imperialistic, individualistic, and democratic seldom meet us in absolute contrast. No individualist ever succeeds in cutting himself off completely from his fellows, or even in staying all the time as much cut off as in his most solitary moments. Even the most convinced imperialist is sometimes visited with questionings as to the wisdom and justice of his Church's decrees. As for democracy, that remains still an aspiration for most of us, the description of the kind of thing we would like to be and to do if we could realize our highest ideal. Nevertheless, the types are real types, and they are

an organization which enables it to deal effectively with the new problems of the present and of the future. No one of the three recognizes democratic religion as an original and independent type.

Of all the writers on religious clasification with whom I am acquainted, Professor Hauter comes nearest to the classification here suggested. He sees clearly that there is need of a new category to describe the type of religion towards which modern Protestantism is tending. But he does not himself suggest that category or define the characteristics of the religion it is designed to express. Cf. his suggestive essay, " Le problème sociologique du Protestantisme," *Revue d'Histoire et de Philosophie religieuses*, Jan.–Feb., 1923. " Thus the vision of a new society appears upon the horizon, a society which is neither gregarious [*i.e.* dominated by the herd instinct], nor sectarian. It is not gregarious, since it is based upon a fully developed individualism ; it is not sectarian, for the individual and society do not seek to escape from each other : on the contrary, they seek each other, and together form but a single whole. Nor is this society a synthesis of individualistic society and collective society. With reference to each of these alternatives it is a new type of society. We have as yet no name to characterize it. This as yet undefined social form is the hidden ideal of Protestantism " (*op. cit.* p. 50).

sufficiently distinct to serve a useful purpose in definition.[1]

Let me make clear at the outset that I do not propose this classification as a *substitute* for other possible classifications, but as a *supplement*. The contrasts in the character of the individual religious life pointed out by psychologists are real contrasts, and they are important contrasts.

[1] On the meaning of the term "type," cf. Jung, *op. cit.* pp. 11, 686. Professor Jung distinguishes two tendencies in human nature which he names respectively "introversion" and "extraversion." The introvert concentrates his attention on what goes on within him—his own subjective states and experiences; whereas the extravert is most interested in external objects. The contrast is never an absolute one, since both tendencies are present to some degree in every normal human being; but it is sufficiently marked to serve as a useful principle of classification. Professor Jung believes that it is possible to distinguish further subdivisions within each of these main groups, according to the greater or less prominence of certain dominant functions, such as thought, feeling, perception (*Empfinden*), intuition (*op. cit.* p. 12). Other psychologists (*e.g.* Trotter) point out other contrasts, such as that between the stable and the unstable type, *i.e.* the man who holds rigidly to a single conclusion after it has once been adopted, and the man who adapts himself readily to new conditions. Tansley (*op. cit.* p. 102), combining Trotter's classification with Jung's, arrives at four main classes—the stable extravert, the unstable extravert, the stable introvert, the unstable introvert. It would be interesting to inquire how the social classification here suggested relates itself to these psychological classifications. Will it appear that the imperialists and democrats to whom our study will introduce us are predominantly of the extravert type, whereas the individualists are introverts? Shall we say that the imperialist is a stable extravert, whereas the democrat is an unstable extravert? Can the difference between the sectarian (cf. p. 125) and the more radical individualist be described by saying that the former is a stable introvert, while the latter is of the unstable variety? Into these interesting but elusive speculations we cannot enter here.

Other differences of far-reaching significance are due to changes in the intellectual and social environment.[1] These differences modify the social attitudes we have distinguished in important and instructive ways, but they do not supersede them. Indeed, the true significance of these other contrasts becomes apparent only when they are studied from this new angle.

A word may be said finally of the choice of the names. In spite of possibilities of misunderstanding, which it must be left for following chapters to remove, the terms " individualism " and " democracy " perhaps sufficiently explain themselves. But the choice of the term " imperialism " may require some justification. Would not institutional religion be a more natural and less misleading word for what we have in mind ? The answer is that institutional religion is too wide for our purpose. It includes forms of tribal and national religion which have no universal religious significance. But imperialism, as the name implies, has the missionary outlook. It aspires to be, it believes that it has the power to become, the religion of mankind. It corresponds, therefore, in the range of its interests with

[1] Such is the difference between a static conception of religion and one that makes room for progress. Even more fundamental is the difference between the type of religion which conceives of God in terms of moral personality, and so conserves, and even enhances, the familiar social and ethical values, and that which expresses the relation between God and man in terms of absolute contrast, and therefore can give no intelligible account of the content of the religious experience.

the other two terms with which we have contrasted it, and will serve better than any other to introduce us to the study of the type it is used to designate.

In choosing the terms imperialism, individualism, and democracy to designate types of religious experience it need hardly be said that we do not intend to pass any moral judgment on the types thus designated, certainly not at the outset. We are not implying that imperialistic religion is bad religion, and democratic religion good religion. That may or may not prove to be the case. We are using the terms as simple descriptions of obvious and incontrovertible facts. We have chosen them because they help us to understand things as they are; and this is the place at which all sound criticism must begin.

I believe that this effort to lay the foundation for criticism in knowledge registers one of the significant moral advances of our time. Whatever else we may decide we ought to do with the types from which we differ, we are coming to see that at least we ought to understand them. And when I say, to understand them, I do not mean simply in the intellectual sense. I mean that we ought to *appreciate* them. It is not enough to know as a matter of fact what men think and what they do. We must learn to understand how they feel, and why they feel so. To do this takes patient study, and long-continued discipline. Above all, it requires ripe experience of life. Before I have the right to judge my neighbour, I must in some true sense *become* my neighbour. I must see with his eyes, and think with his thoughts, and feel with his heart. Only then have I won the right to differ from him.

This does not mean that I must surrender my right to differ. Our plea for sympathy is not a plea for indifference. Rather is it a plea for the conditions which alone make just judgment possible. Because the three types of religion of which we have spoken are all of them likely to be permanent, it does not follow that they are all of them equally useful or all of them equally true. There is a moral problem in classification as well as an intellectual problem. We have not only to account for these different forms of religion. We have to evaluate them. Granting that they are here, and here to stay, what shall we do with them? We cannot belong to all of them at the same time. At least such an achievement is possible only at rare intervals and to a virtuoso in sympathy. We must choose between them. And, having chosen, we must decide what our attitude shall be to the individuals and to the types from which we differ. I shall have something to say on this point later on.[1] All that I wish here to do is to interpret the spirit in which we should approach our study. It will be, I trust, a spirit of enlightened sympathy. But it will be at the same time a spirit of serious responsibility. We shall spare no pains to understand. We should not forget, that when we have understood, we must act.

[1] Cf. especially Chapter VI.

3

CHAPTER II

RELIGION AS PERSONAL EXPERIENCE AND AS HISTORIC PROCESS

1. *Imperialism, Individualism, and Democracy as Recurrent Religious Types*

IN the last chapter we reviewed some of the explanations which have been given of the fact of variation in religion and pointed out wherein they were inadequate. We agreed that the method of approach which gave most promise of success was psychological, and that to account for the puzzling phenomena in religious history we must be able to explain the emergence and persistence, side by side, of contrasted types of religious experience. We selected for special study three such types which have played a great rôle in religious history, which for the purposes of the present investigation we agreed to call imperialism, individualism, and democracy. In the present chapter we must examine this classification more carefully in the light of the fundamental conceptions which it presupposes.

We saw that there are three possible attitudes which the individual may take toward organized society. He may accept it as it is ; he may

34

reject it altogether ; he may try to improve it.
These attitudes have their counterparts in religious experience. There are people who are
conservative in their attitude toward existing
institutions who accept them as they are, and
who yield them unquestioning allegiance. The
victory of their party or of their Church is the
form in which their own personality finds its
most complete and satisfying expression. They
can conceive of no more gratifying success, no
more rewarding experience than to have taken
part in helping to secure this victory. Their
judgment of other men is determined in the
same way. Acquaintances are good or bad,
worthy of praise or of blame, according as they
confess the same allegiance, and yield the same
obedience. For to their minds, no other good
compares with the triumph of their Church or
of their nation. They do not recognize any
rights which exist independently of it. They do
not shrink from any act which is necessary to
make it secure. We have called such an attitude
of mind imperialism, and the type of religion to
which it gives rise imperialistic religion.

There are others whose attitude to society is
just the reverse. They cannot find anywhere in
the existing institutions of society what completely—or even measurably—satisfies their sense
of truth and of beauty. They are revolted by
the compromises which organized society asks of
those who live under it. They feel their inner
freedom impaired, the full development of their

God-given personality thwarted. They are in quest of another world where they can develop each in his way—an unseen reality in communion with which they may find self-fulfilment. They are individualists in the sense that they make the realization of God's presence in their own individual personality the *summum bonum*, and for this are ready to sacrifice all else, even the most sacred human relationships. They are in the world, but not of the world. Their religion asks for God and the soul—nothing more.

And there are still others whose attitude differs from both of these. They agree with the individualist in his criticism of existing society. Like him, they insist upon the autonomy of the free spirit. Rather than surrender this they will make every sacrifice. But the freedom which they claim for themselves they are willing to grant to others. They do not think that they possess the whole truth, or that they can ever attain it by themselves. Although they may find much to criticize in existing society, they are not despondent as to its longer future. They are convinced that social institutions are capable of improvement, and they ask nothing better than to join in the effort to improve them. They know that this will be a long and arduous task, and that their own generation will not live to see it finished. But they are confident that in the end it can be accomplished. Such an attitude we have called democratic, and the type of religion to which it gives rise, democratic religion.

With so much by way of preface we may begin the more detailed consideration of our theme. We have called the types of social attitude which we have been contrasting religious. It may fairly be asked how we justify the use of this word. To do this it will be necessary to go back a little and to define some of the fundamental conceptions which any study of specific religious phenomena presupposes.

2. *What is meant by Religion. Its Threefold Aspect as Belief, Feeling, and Action*

And first religion itself. Significant progress has been registered at this initial point. Not long ago almost every writer upon religion thought it necessary to call attention to the impossibility of securing any wide agreement as to what religion is.[1] Recent monographs on religious subjects yield a different result. We are struck by the extent of their agreement in defining religion.[2] We now feel sure that we really know

[1] Thus Mr. Benjamin Kidd in his widely read book, *Social Evolution* (1894), begins by giving his readers a long list of definitions of religion, extending over two or three pages. After having thus demonstrated by the example of the greatest masters that it is impossible to agree upon any single definition of religion, he proceeds confidently to add his own.

[2] To justify this statement in detail would require more space than is at present at our disposal. It is sufficient to say that the differences of which many writers on religion make so much are due less to fundamental disagreement as to what religion is, than to varying emphasis upon one or other of the different aspects of its many-sided life.

what religion is, and we are able to distinguish it with reasonable clearness from other phases of man's experience. We have learned that it is both broader and narrower than has been conventionally supposed. Religion, like other living things, may create a shell which can be left behind when life has departed. But religion may be most alive before the shell has appeared. Religious institutions are the shells of religion. But if we understand them for what they are, we shall find that they are not unworthy of our study and our respect.

In what follows we shall understand by religion that phase of man's experience, individual or social, which leads him to look up to a higher power and to confess his dependence on it, to offer that higher power the homage of reverence or awe which we call worship, and to take such action as he believes will attract the favour of the deity or conform to his will. The existing forms of religion differ widely in the way they conceive the object of their worship, the feelings which that worship calls forth, and the activities through which it finds expression. But every living religion, whatever its character in detail, assumes the existence of a deity, professes to bring about a personal relationship between the deity and his worshippers, and provides an outlet for that relation in some appropriate form of action.

These three aspects of the life of religion, the beliefs it presupposes, the feelings it engenders, and the activities it calls forth, are all intimately related. They act and react upon one another in countless ways, yet the correspondence between the three is never perfect, and all three are affected in definite and recognizable ways by the shell to which we have already referred.

3. *The Permanent and the Variable in the Idea of Deity. God as the Realized Ideal*

We have said that the ideas of deity differ widely. We Western Christians with our theistic tradition are so accustomed to think of the word " God " as if it had a definite and unmistakable connotation, that some of our most eminent writers on religion have scarcely thought it necessary to define what they meant by the term. They have assumed that the word God would mean the same thing to everybody, and all that was necessary was to determine whether one believed in God or not. But it needs little acquaintance with the history of religion to show us that such a procedure is too crude to be practical. In the past the term deity has stood for the most widely separated ideas, and this is true to-day. Every change in man's intellectual and social environment has been reflected in his thinking about God. The Deity has been thought of as like man, and as unlike him ; as personal and supra-personal ; as one and many ; as absolute and limited ; as indifferent to man and as keenly concerned for his welfare ; as entering into our experiences in sympathy, and by His very nature incapable of suffering. These contrasts are found within the same religion. Two centuries after the writer to the Hebrews found the chief glory of Christianity in the fact that the divine high priest who gave us our most complete and trustworthy revelation of God could be " touched with the feeling of our infirmities " and was " at all points tempted like as we are." [1] a Christian apologist attempted to win the respect of his contemporaries by the following description of God.[2]

" If you do not refuse to hear what we think, we are so far from attributing to God bodily lineaments that we fear to ascribe to so great an object even the graces of the mind, and the very virtues in which to excel is hardly granted to a few. For who can speak of God as brave, as constant, as moderate, as wise. Nay, who can say that He knows anything, that He understands, that He acts with foresight, that He directs the determination of His actions towards definite ends of duty. These are human goods, and as opposed to vices deserve a laudable reputation. But who is there so dull of heart and stupid as to call God great in human goods, or to speak of the surpassing excellence of His name as if it consisted in a freedom from the stain of vices. Whatever you can say of God, whatever you can conceive in silent thought, passes into a human

---

[1] Heb. iv. 15.

[2] Arnobius, *adv. Gentes*, iii. 19, quoted in Mansel, *Limits of Religious Thought*, 5th ed., 1867, p. xxii.

sense, and is corrupted thereby. Nothing can
properly signify and denote Him which is expressed in terms of human speech for human
uses. There is but one way in which man can
understand with certainty concerning the nature
of God, and that is to know and feel that nothing
can be expressed concerning Him in mortal
speech."

Yet through all these contrasts, certain stable
elements persist. The God of living religion is
always conceived as really existing. He is always
in some sense superior to His worshipper, the
object of reverence and awe. He is always
regarded as holding some personal relationship
to His worshipper which has practical consequences for life. This consciousness of personal
relationship is of the very essence of the religious
experience. It marks the dividing line between
philosophy and religion. " Religion begins," has
said an acute critic, " when I address the Deity
by the personal pronoun." The philosopher
may believe in *a* God : the religious man cries
" *My* God."

The sense of a personal relationship to a
higher power leading to worship, which we have
seen to be the characteristic feature of the religious
experience, may be illustrated in many utterances
which are not commonly regarded as religious
at all. We may cite two examples which are
all the more instructive because they are taken
from the writings of men who have broken with
the accepted forms of organized religion. The

first is from a poet, the second from a man who is internationally known as an ethical teacher. Both have been repeatedly characterized by religious people as unbelievers.

Our first witness is Shelley, and the quotation is from his Hymn on Intellectual Beauty.

> "Spirit of Beauty, that dost consecrate
>   With thine own hues all thou dost shine upon
>   Of human thought or form, where art thou gone ?
> Why dost thou pass away and leave our state,
> This dim vast vale of tears, vacant and desolate.
>
>   .   .   .   .
>
> I vowed that I would dedicate my powers
>   To thee and thine. Have I not kept my vow ?
>   With beating heart and streaming eyes, even now
> I call the phantoms of a thousand hours
> Each from his voiceless grave ; they have in visioned bowers
>   Of studious zeal or love's delight
>   Outwatched with me the envious night,
> They know that never joy illumed my brow
>   Unlinked with hope that thou wouldest free
>   This world from its dark slavery,
>   That thou—O awful Loveliness,
> Would'st give whate'er these words cannot express."

This is a typically religious utterance. It has all the marks of the experience we have been defining, the belief in the existence of a higher power, the upward look, the sense of reverence and worship, and above all the consciousness of a personal relationship which finds expression in a definite act of will.

The second witness is Dr. Felix Adler, the eminent teacher and scholar, founder and head of the Society of Ethical Culture in New York ;

and the quotation is from his little book called
The Religion of Duty.[1]

"There is something in religion," says Dr.
Adler, "besides its doctrines, its symbols, and its
ceremonies. There is something underlying,
which we cannot afford to lose, and do not wish
to lose, without which our lives would be poor
and miserable indeed. That which is ever-
lastingly precious in religion is the conviction
that life is worth while, because there is something going forward in the universe which is
essentially worth while, something shaping itself
towards that

> One far-off divine event
> Toward which the whole creation moves.

"Our individual lives are so poor, so petty,
and so meaningless that there must be something
greater which our lives subserve in order to
make them worth the while, something infinitely
beautiful and holy, working itself out in things
which may be served by our poor lives. We
need the conviction that this world is not a
colossal loom on which the shuttle of chance
weaves the garment of unreason and despair ;
that our ideals are not mere wishes, with no surety
of fulfilment, but that at the heart of things there
is that which will make them real."

"There is that at the heart of things which
will make our wishes real." "There is something greater than we which may be served by

[1] New York, 1905, p. 1.

our poor lives." It is the characteristic language of religion. This "greater than we," this "infinitely beautiful and holy," through which our lives may find fulfilment, and yet which can use us for ends outside ourselves, religion knows as God. Define it as you will. Be as negative in your description as Arnobius. Say, as Dr. Adler says further on in the book from which I have already quoted: "This higher Being is not like a man, is not He or She or It, did not make the world as a carpenter makes a table or as an architect builds a house. In the attempt to describe this Being language faints, imagination grows dizzy, thought is paralyzed";[1]—still if you have in your experience these four elements which we have described, the sense of reality, the upward look, the spirit of worship, the personal identification, you are a religious man.

We may put it in this way. All the people in the world without exception have ideals of some kind. There are moments when they conceive of something better and more desirable than the crude present in which they are living. There is something they would like to have. There is something they would like to do. There is something they would like to be. These pictures of the mind, these standards by which we shape life, not according to its present facts, but according to our standard of value we call ideals. All men, I repeat, have ideals of some kind. But to some they are luxuries. One would

[1] P. 39.

like to have them if one could, but one can dispense with them if one must.   If one must choose between one's ideals and one's livelihood, the ideal must go.   To others their ideals are necessities.   They would rather fail in search of them than succeed without them.   The man whose ideals are luxuries is irreligious.   The man whose ideals are necessaries is religious.   God is the name we give to our realized ideal, and in all theistic religions He is the one through whom we may hope to realize the ideal in ourselves, and in our world.   Religious people differ in the way they define this ideal, and in the vividness of their consciousness of its present realization.

4. *Corresponding Contrasts in the Religious Attitude. Legalistic and Mystical Religion*

These differences in the conception of the object of worship are paralleled by corresponding differences of feeling in the worshippers.   In man's emotional life, as well as in his beliefs and in his actions, the story of religion is the story of contrast.   Fear played a great rôle in primitive religion.   Religion was a device for propitiating an angry or at least a moody deity.   Only in later stages does the sense of intimacy emerge, and God begin to be thought of as one who loves His worshippers.   When Jesus spoke His great word about friendship, He set a new standard for religious relationships.   " No longer do I call you servants ; for the servant knoweth not

Peruvian king who is said to have remarked
that the sun could not be a god, because if that
were true he would not get up in the same place
every morning and go to bed in the same place
every night. To simple-minded people, freedom
and arbitrariness are synonyms. Only later do
we discover that the highest freedom fulfils itself
through law. This change in the nature of man's
moral standards is accompanied by corresponding
changes in his emotional experience, which reflect
themselves in the nature of his worship.

5. *Different Ways in which Religion finds Expression
in Action. Ceremonial and Ethical Religion.
The Permanent Basis of Sacramentarianism*

But if man's thoughts and his feelings change
in religion this is still more true of his actions.
No one of all the many things he does but may
be given a religious significance. No change in
social customs or in ethical standards but has
its corresponding effect upon his religious activity.
Here we need only call attention to two contrasts of fundamental and permanent importance.
The first is the contrast between those activities
which take place within the spirit of man himself,
like prayer, meditation, worship in the narrow
sense, and those outward acts like sacrifice, and
church-going, which can be shared by others.
The second is the contrast between those acts
which are regarded as religious in a peculiar sense,
like preaching, prayer, and the observance of

sacraments, and that wider range of activities, like charity, helpfulness, and social reform which differ from corresponding acts by irreligious people simply in the different motive which inspires them.

On the first of these contrasts, that between inward and outward activity, we need not comment ; for it is only the repetition in the field of religion of a distinction which is everywhere familiar in our lives. But of the second a word may be said. The contrast between religious acts in the narrow or technical sense and that wider range of activity which is often called religious, is one of the most familiar in the whole history of religion. It corresponds roughly to the difference between what is known as ceremonial and ethical religion. Ceremonial religion is the name we give to a class of activities which have the deity for their object in a direct and immediate fashion, and are commonly believed to have been definitely prescribed by him. Ethical religion, on the other hand, includes all those acts which express a man's relation to his fellow-men. Ethics becomes religious in the measure that these relations are regarded as a subject of the divine interest, and as a means through which the divine favour may be secured or the divine purpose furthered.

The whole field of ceremonial religion presents almost insuperable difficulty to numbers of earnest people to-day. At no point is the contrast between the inner feelings which we have called religious, and the acts which are supposed

4

to express them more glaring. At no point is the remoteness of much that we call religion from the world around us so patent and repelling. It may help us to recall how ceremonial religion probably began, and what are the different attitudes which men have taken toward it.

It seems likely that what we to-day call ceremonial religion had its origin in a time when the deity was regarded as one individual among others. We are apt to forget that our unified world view, with its single Deity and its universal law, was a comparatively late discovery. Our ancestors did not live in one great world, but in many little worlds, and each world was presided over by its own deity or deities. Ceremonial religion was the code which prescribed the kind of acts which each of these deities demanded. It defined man's duty to his god, as tribal custom prescribed his duty to his chief and to his peers. Violation of the first was sin, of the second crime. And the things the god required were not different in kind from the things the chief required. Homage, gifts, the observance of a prescribed ritual,—we can find parallels all the way along. When man sacrificed he gave the gods the part they wanted of the things which he had, in just the same simple and unquestioning spirit that he gave to his chief.

But as time went on, and man's horizon broadened, this naive attitude became impossible. The many worlds had given place to one world, and the many gods to one God. And with the

expanding sense of God's power had come a new
conception of His nature and His interest.   He
was no longer an individual among individuals.
He was the creator and sustainer of the universe.
He prescribed the standard of conduct for mankind.   He was the guardian of the moral law.
In such a situation the old explanation of religious
ceremonial had lost its meaning.   And yet the
ceremonial was there, and about it all sorts of
solemn sanctions had gathered.   It was not only
maintained by the interest of the priests who lived
by it.   It corresponded to some felt need in the
lives that had grown accustomed to it.

In this situation there were two possible ways
out, both of which were taken.   One might retain
the ceremonial unchanged, and justify it by a
philosophy of authority.   One might say : " The
Deity cares nothing for these acts in themselves.
How can the God of all the earth, in Himself all-
sufficient, be profited by what men can do ?   God
is so far above man that not even our highest
thought can penetrate the mysteries of the
divine nature.   If man is to reach God, it must
be by some method of God's own devising.
Such a method is given us in ceremonial religion.
In the ritual, and sacraments of the prescribed
code, acts meaningless in themselves, and making
use of materials in themselves indifferent, God
has provided a channel through which His
supernatural grace may be communicated to
man.   It is not necessary to understand how
this communication can be made ; it is even

impossible to do so. But no one who in reverent spirit approaches the Sacrament can doubt that such communication has, in fact, been made. The new experience of peace and power which it brings to pass is its own sufficient evidence." This general method of explaining and justifying ceremonial religion, we may call, for want of a better term, Sacramentarianism.[1]

Yet potent as are the considerations thus suggested they would not of themselves be sufficient to account for the power and persistence of sacramentarian religion. Sacramentarianism has many roots. It witnesses to man's deep-seated belief in the spiritual significance of material things. It expresses his desire to find a religious meaning in the concrete, in things which can be seen and handled. The Sacrament speaks a language which can be understood by simple people who find the doctrines of religion too abstract to meet their spiritual needs. Yet at the same time it lends itself to a symbolic interpretation which has a very different theoretical basis.

This different basis is presupposed in the second method of dealing with ceremonial religion. One may retain the ritual of the old religion, but give it a symbolic meaning. One

[1] This use of the term is a narrower one than the more general use on p. 10. In the latter sense any one who makes the sacrament central in his religious life may be called a sacramentarian. Here the term is applied to those who justify their emphasis upon the Sacrament by a particular theory of its nature—the theory, namely, that it is the channel of a mysterious supernatural grace, not accessible in any other way.

may see in it a dramatization of universal truths, a parabolic representation of the principles of ethical religion in which alone God is really interested and through which alone the soul communes acceptably with Him. According to this view the Sacrament is not a mysterious rite working *ex opere operato*, through which an otherwise inaccessible divine grace is conveyed to man. It is the symbol of an ever-present divine activity, the means through which the soul, refreshed by contemplation of the divine wisdom and goodness may be better furnished for the daily task of fraternity.

These contrasts, and others which might be added, are important for our understanding of historic religion. But they need not detain us here. The three great types which are the subject of our present study, imperialism, individualism, and democracy, have other roots and can be studied by themselves. They are independent of these other contrasts, and combine with them in a great variety of ways. But they cannot be fully understood till we carry our analysis of religion one step further, and take note of its social manifestations.

6. *The Significance of the Church as the Institution of Religion. Its Fivefold Function in Worship, Education, Discipline, Service, and Propaganda*

For religion, like all permanent human interests, is a social affair. It develops its appropriate organization. It functions through institutions which we call Churches, which in turn are divided, as we have seen, into sects and schools, which may in time become independent units, with further subdivisions of their own.

Again, religion has a history. In the course of this history the existing forms are constantly being modified. In the process of change emerge the contrasted social complexes we call the religions. Some of these have their origin in the remote past, and find their bond of union in tribal or national tradition. Others are due to the initiative of an individual who stamps his character upon the whole succeeding history. Buddhism, Christianity, Mohammedanism, to a less extent Judaism, are examples of such founded religions. The same is true of many of the lesser religious units. One thinks of Francis and of Loyola among the Catholics, of Wesley and of General Booth among the Protestants. But all alike—founded or ancestral religions—are social forms of religion. They are churchly religions. They have their Bibles, their temples, their ritual, their priesthood. They have their laws to which they seek to secure allegiance, their schools by which they try to discipline character. Many of them are missionary religions. Some of them aspire to be world religions. And within themselves they are divided in the manner which we have already described. When these inter-religious divisions make organization their principle of difference

we call them denominations ; when they find
it in agreement in a body of teaching we call
them schools or parties.

The contrast we are to study in these pages
emerges in relation to men's attitude to these
different forms of religious organization. Imperialism, individualism, and democracy are
either forms of churchly religion, or can only be
understood as a protest against it.

It will help, therefore, to provide us with a
test for intelligent comparison, if we remind
ourselves briefly of the purpose which Churches
fulfil, and the ways in which they function.
Every Church worthy the name has at least five
main functions which it discharges in the life
of its worshippers. It is the organ of their
common worship. It is the school in which they
are instructed in the meaning of their religion.
It is the instrument of their moral discipline.
It is the agency through which they combine
for common service. Finally, it is the means
through which the tenets of their religion are
propagated.

The Church is primarily the organ of common
worship. The temple is the characteristic religious building, found in all countries and in all
ages. The priesthood has as its most important
function to mediate between the worshippers
and their deity, and to lead them in the common
acts through which that worship may find
appropriate expression. No change in the theory
of religion can displace worship from its central

place. It is as truly first in the silent meeting of the Friends, as in the elaborate ritual of the most gorgeous cathedral. To make men realize that God is, and that He is the rewarder of them that diligently seek Him, to show them the ways in which this consciousness may be aroused and stimulated, this is the unique and distinctive function of the Church, the world over.

The Church is also the school in which men are instructed in the meaning of their religion. In primitive religion this instruction was very simple. It had to do with the accepted rites and ceremonies, and how they were to be rightly performed. But on a higher grade of culture, instruction becomes an increasingly important function of the Church. The sermon is added to the sacrament. The Sunday school takes its place beside the secular school, and the theological seminary beside the law school and the medical school. Especially in highly organized religions like Christianity and Buddhism, which presuppose on the part of their adherents a considerable degree of knowledge, the function of the Church as a teacher of doctrine becomes important.

With teaching goes discipline. This is notably true of the ethical religions. But every religion which has a Church assumes at least in theory some responsibility for the conduct of its adherents. There are some things which no Church can tolerate, such as the profanation of its temples, or the neglect of its ceremonies. In those

religions which think of the Deity as a moral
being, the source of public law and the guardian
of public morals, the Church is concerned with
the daily lives of its worshippers, and may seek
to control these by Church court or confessional.
In mystical religions, where attention is concentrated upon the relation between the individual
soul and God, the discipline may be self-inflicted,
and the assistance of the Church be given through
the code of rules which it puts into the hands
of the devotee, in his search for God.

Discipline is accompanied by service. The
Church is not only responsible for developing the
character of its worshippers. It has work for
them to do. The nature and motives of this work
may differ widely, but in all the ethical religions
at least, the holiness which the Deity requires of
His worshippers includes right conduct toward
their fellow-men. Micah's famous word is typical
of a dominant tendency in religion. " He
hath showed thee, O man, what is good ; and
what doth Jehovah require of thee, but to love
justice, and to show mercy, and to walk humbly
before thy God ? " [1] Churches exist among other
things to show man what God requires, and to
help them to meet that requirement.

Propaganda, finally, is an important churchly
function. All the greater religions are missionary religions, and their Churches are the
agencies through which this missionary work
is carried on. Different methods are used, and

[1] vi. 8.

the extent of the demand upon the intelligence
and the will of the convert varies. Some religions are satisfied with very little. An outward
act like baptism or the burning of incense is
enough. Others are not content without an
inner acceptance of the doctrines and ideals of
the faith. To secure this acceptance elaborate
methods have been devised, and a voluminous
literature has been brought into existence. But
underlying all this is a common conviction—
the conviction that the truths of religion have
universal significance, and that a believer should
do his utmost to make them known.

This analysis will make it easier for us to
appreciate the significance of the contrasted
types which we have distinguished. The representatives of each approach the tasks of religion
in their own way. Each group worships, teaches,
disciplines, ministers, evangelizes in the way that
is most natural and congenial. By studying
them at work at this fivefold task, we can understand the genius of the three types of religious
experience which we have called imperialism,
individualism, and democracy.

7. *The Creative Element in Religion. The Contribution of History to Religion. Institutional
Religion as at once Enfranchising and Limiting*

One further contrast needs brief mention in
order to bring all the data before us ; and that is
the contrast between religion as a creator of new

values and as a conservator of values which already exist.

Professor Hocking, in his illuminating book, *The Meaning of God in Human Experience*,[1] has called attention to the creative element in the religious experience. Wherever we meet living religion we are conscious of a sense of power. Energies are released, insights achieved, barriers broken down. Windows are opened into a new world. Doors are discovered through which the spirit at the end of its former resources may move forward into ampler activities.

" I can do all things in Him that strengtheneth me " ; [2] " I came that they may have life, and may have it abundantly." [3] This fresh and virile note meets us most clearly in the great masters. But it is present wherever the individual comes into possession of a vital religious experience. There are moments in the life of every truly religious person when he becomes vividly conscious of the presence of God, and these moments are accompanied by a sense of inner satisfaction and by a certainty which is its own best evidence. This irresistible consciousness of the presence of God is the psychological basis of belief in miracle.[4] It is a recurrent element in religion, found in all ages and in all religions.

But this creative element is present in different

---

[1] New Haven, 1912.   [2] Phil. iv. 13.   [3] John x. 10.
[4] Cf. W. Adams Brown, " The Permanent Significance of Miracle for Religion," *Harvard Theological Review*, July 1915, p. 314 seq.

individuals in different degree, and in the same individual in different degree at different times. There are some persons who never seem to lose their sense of the presence of God. They are conscious day by day of receiving fresh insight and renewed power from above. And what they have received they are able to impart. Others who touch them catch the contagion of their faith, and are lifted above themselves to new heights of vision and happiness. We call these rare spirits prophets or saints. They are able not only to realize God for themselves, but to mediate His presence to others. The words they speak live after them. The standards they set mould later lives.

The historic religions, at least the greater and best known of them, owe their existence as separate social entities to the contagion of such creative religious personalities. To be sure each of these creative spirits used earlier materials. Gautama took for granted the older religions of India. Mohammed borrowed both from Judaism and from Christianity. Jesus was the heir of the prophets. But each saw God for himself, and each was able to create fresh vision in others. Those who came after looked up to them as masters, and by touching them found power to see God for themselves. Their memory, handed down in reverent tradition, creates similar experiences in succeeding generations.

In this process of transmission an indispensable part is played by the institution. We saw

that institutions are the means which society
uses to protect its expanding spiritual life.
Institutions perpetuate the life-work of individuals
by creating forms through which those who come
after may have convenient access to their distinctive message.   They guard the spiritual gains
of the past.   They safeguard the nascent spiritual
life of the present.   Churches are the shells of
religion.   They give social sanction to beliefs and
practices which have proved useful.   They set
a standard by which to direct energies which
without such direction might go astray.   Without
their help religion could not be perpetuated.
But this service is rendered at a price.   The
shell protects the expanding life within, but
there comes a time when it also cramps it.   There
are moments when the fetters placed upon
freedom by institutional life are heavier than
can be borne.   There is then no alternative but
to break the shell.   But the newly-won freedom
will not remain long unprotected.   It must make
a shell of its own in order to endure.

Happily it is not always necessary that a
break should take place.   The older an institution grows, the more of value it accumulates.   As
it moves through the centuries it becomes possessed of great traditions and a great literature.
These traditions and this literature may stimulate
insights which will express themselves in new
ways.   Some of the freest spirits who have ever
lived have remained all their lives loyal sons of
the Church, and even those who have broken

away owe their impulse to her teaching. The Church has been the mother of the Reformers.

This double effect of history as at once enfranchising and enslaving may be studied to a greater or less extent in all the greater religions. Historic Christianity—to take the illustration most familiar to us—has been at once the nursery of free spirits and their prison. The institution which has preserved our greatest gifts—the knowledge of the Master, the illumination and stimulus of the Bible, the communion of saints —has altered, often debased them. This has not been done deliberately, but as part of the inevitable process of shell-building. The new values come to men in specific situations, and they react accordingly. They carry over into a new religion their familiar habits and beliefs. They carry over also their differences of temperament. One man reacts to Jesus in one way, and another in another. And the institutions of the developing religion are modified accordingly.

Yet through all the vicissitudes of the history, the life within makes itself felt ; not always quickly or effectively, but unmistakably. Each brings his own needs and his own capacities to the great tradition which the Church hands down, and each finds in it the thing which meets his deepest need. The imperialist sees in the founder of his religion the head of the Church, the sovereign of the universe, the judge before whom every knee must bow. The individualist sees in him a hero who has dared to break with

Church and State and stand alone for the truth. The democrat sees in him the first-born of many brethren, the founder and leader of a new society of helpfulness.   But each is persuaded that in his own type of experience he has met *God*, and received the guidance he needs for his own life.

CHAPTER III

IMPERIALISTIC RELIGION: ITS NATURE AND VARIETIES

1. *The Roman Catholic Church as an Example of Imperialistic Religion. The Church as Mediator between God and Man*

OF the three types of religion contrasted in previous chapters, the one which we have called imperialistic is easiest to describe. The imperialist believes that he serves God best when he submits himself completely to the control and service of a definite organization whose triumph in the world he identifies with God's will. To understand the imperialist's religion, therefore, we must know what institution commands his allegiance, and what that institution requires of him.

One characteristic common to all forms of imperialistic religion strikes us at the outset. What the institution asks of its adherents is not merely their personal obedience, but that they should make its requirements their standard for judging other men. There are forms of institutional religion which are content to be tribal or national religions, without denying the right of

other religions to exist by their side. Imperialism
is a missionary religion. Its devotees not only
find satisfaction in submission for themselves ;
they believe that it is best for every one. Imperialism makes heroes and martyrs. It has made
tyrants and persecutors as well.

When we look for examples of imperialistic
religion we think most naturally of ultramontane
Roman Catholicism which claims world - wide
dominion and demands absolute submission.
This religion has lasted for the best part of a
millennium and in its beginnings goes back many
centuries further. Apparently it is quite as
strong as ever and a factor to be reckoned with
in the life of to-day. We can hardly find a better
object-lesson in imperialism than the Roman
Catholic Church.

Many centuries ago a remarkable meeting
took place at Canossa. It was an interview
between an Emperor and a Pope. The Emperor
was the most notable prince in Europe — a
potentate who held a position of unexampled
dignity and power. But he came to Canossa
as a suppliant in penitential garb to prostrate
himself before a minister of religion and beg his
forgiveness and absolution. It was not force of
arms alone which brought him there, but some
intangible power of the Spirit. To understand
imperialistic religion we must study this power,
and learn what it meant both to him who
exercised it and to him upon whom it was
exercised.

5

single act of faith by which a Catholic accepts
the voice of the Church as the voice of God.[1]
The one sin which for the Catholic admits of no
forgiveness is unbelief, and unbelief means unwillingness to accept at the full value and in the
sense that the Church intends, whatever its
authorized representatives may teach.

Newman's testimony on this point is illuminating. It occurs in the significant passage in the
Apologia, in which he describes his mental attitude after he had made the act of submission.

" People say that the doctrine of transubstantiation is difficult to believe. I did not
believe the doctrine till I was a Catholic. I had
no difficulty in believing it as soon as I believed
that the Catholic Roman Church was the oracle
of God, and that she had declared this doctrine
part of the original revelation. It is difficult,
impossible to imagine, I grant, but how is it
difficult to believe? Yet Macaulay thought it so
difficult to believe that he had need of a believer
in it, as eminent as Sir Thomas More, before he
could bring himself to conceive that the Catholics
of an enlightened age could resist ' the over-
whelming force of the argument against it.'
' Sir Thomas More,' he says, ' is one of the
choice specimens of wisdom and virtue—and

---

[1] The difference between the two attitudes may be represented by the two contrasted formulæ, *Credo ut intelligam* and
Credo quia impossibile est, which may be rendered respectively :
" I make the act of submission, because that is the condition
of understanding." ; " I make the act of submission, because it
is of the very nature of faith to accept that which to the natural
reason is incredible."

the doctrine of transubstantiation is a kind of proof charge. A faith which stands that test will stand any test.' But for myself, I cannot indeed prove it. I cannot tell how it is, but I say, ' Why should it not be ? What's to hinder it ? What do I know of substance or matter ? Just as much as the greatest philosophers, and that is nothing at all.' ' So much is this the case '—Newman goes on—' that there is a rising school of philosophy now, which considers phenomena to constitute the whole of our knowledge in physics. The Catholic doctrine leaves phenomena alone. It does not say that the phenomena go ; on the contrary, it says that they remain ; nor does it say that the same phenomena are in several places at once. It deals with what no one on earth knows anything about, the material substances themselves. And in like manner of that majestic article of the Anglican as well as of the Catholic creed, the doctrine of the Trinity in Unity. What do I know of the essence of the divine being ? I know that my abstract idea of three is simply incompatible with my abstract idea of one ; but when I come to the question of concrete fact I have no means of proving that there is not a sense in which one and three may equally be affirmed of the incommunicable God." [1]

In these words scepticism is raised to the dignity of a religious virtue.

But it may well be asked, How does this help us ? What does it profit us to possess the revelation of the transcendent God, if even after

[1] *Apologia pro Vitâ Suâ*, London, 1873, p. 239 seq.

the Church has put us in possession of it, it conveys to our mind no definite and intelligible meaning ? The Catholic answers that God has other ways of imparting Himself than through the mind. He is a God of action ; and that action has taken the form of a series of redemptive deeds which have for their purpose man's salvation. These deeds are in their own nature unintelligible. They are miracles, and as such unpredictable. But these miracles are not isolated and unrelated phenomena. They have succeeded one another in a regular historic succession, and culminated in the creation of an institution which makes possible the contact with God which the soul craves. This contact is mediated through a series of miraculous acts called Sacraments. In the Sacrament the divine grace lays hold of man and transforms him from a child of nature into a being truly supernatural. The centre of these miraculous redemptive acts is the Mass, and all the other sacraments are to be understood either as preparations for it, or as a means of carrying further forward the divine work which it has begun. In the Mass the transcendent miracle of transubstantiation takes place—a miracle through which the believer is enabled to feed upon the very body and blood of his Saviour ; and what is more wonderful still, the divine sacrifice on Calvary is re-presented in bloodless form, and so new merit is created which becomes available for the needs of new generations of sinners.

Clearly, then, nothing is more important to the devout Catholic than faithful attendance upon this central rite of his religion. Here in a very true and literal way he meets God face to face. Here in his own personal life he experiences miracle. " I felt instinctively," once said Tyrrell in an illuminating passage which describes an experience of his pre-Catholic days, " what I long afterwards understood clearly, that the difference between an altar and a Communion table, was infinite." [1]

About this central act of the Catholic worship, there gather a multitude of lesser acts recognized by the Church and carried on with its approval. That only is true worship in the sense in which the devout Catholic understands that term, which the Church has endorsed and which it can control.

2. *The Church as Regulator of Belief. Different Attitudes toward Layman and Specialist*

Such being the God whom the Catholic worships, and such the manner in which his worship is performed, we must next ask how the believer is prepared to worship acceptably. This leads us to consider the function of the Church as a teacher of religion—a function scarcely less important than that of worship itself.

So far as theory is concerned, the Catholic

---

[1] *Autobiography of George Tyrrell*, London, 1912, vol. ii. p. 98.

position is simple. The *ecclesia docens* claims
all education for its field. It makes itself responsible for what its members think all along
the line. They are allowed to read only what
it prescribes. They are expected to study only
where it permits. There is no phase of human
experience, no department of human research to
which in theory at least this principle does not
apply. No phase of contemporary activity,
whether it be economic, political, or social, but
falls within the purview of the Church. The
encyclicals of the Popes would furnish material
for the reconstruction of contemporary history,
and the Papal syllabus of errors would serve as
a convenient introduction to the study of contemporary philosophy. When one realizes how
elusive is human thought, how deep-seated
human curiosity, this claim to bring every
thought into captivity to the obedience of Rome
becomes magnificent in its audacity.

Nor does the theory remain merely a theory.
It is carried out in great detail through an
elaborate machinery. This consists in part of
institutions maintained and controlled by the
Church. These institutions begin with the
parochial school, and continue to the university.
In these institutions the child's course of study
is prescribed from his earliest years, and carried
on through his period of professional study.
But apart from its own schools, the Church has
agencies by which it attempts to control the
thought-life of the Catholic even when he is

educated in secular institutions. The Index of
prohibited books is one cog in this complicated
machine. Some years ago Henri Lasserre, a
devout French Catholic, was cured of a serious
disease by the Virgin of Lourdes. In gratitude
for this signal mercy he conceived the plan of
making a translation of the four Gospels into
modern French, so that the story of the great
healer might be made accessible to the multitudes of his fellow-Catholics in France who
were ignorant of it. The translation was
made and approved by the Church; it had a
success beyond the author's hope. Multitudes
of French Catholics began to read the Gospels
in Lasserre's rendering. The authorities were
alarmed. They did not know whereto this thing
might grow. The *imprimatur* was withdrawn.
Lasserre's book appeared upon the Index, and
its copies disappeared from the book-stores of
France.

But if the Church exercises such strict control
over the reading of the ordinary Roman Catholic,
it applies a very different standard to those whom
it has set apart for its ministry. When the
candidate has been sufficiently tested and his
grounding in the faith has been secured beyond a
doubt, there is no branch of human knowledge
which is not open to him. For the Church has
work to be done in the world of men, and for this
its servants must know men, and the thoughts
of men. In no modern schools is specialization
carried further than in the schools of Rome;

and prescribe what it wishes him to do under conditions which give the best promise of success. Rome is not the only Church which has tried to exercise such control, but it is the only one that has even measurably succeeded. An intelligent Russian was once requested to explain the penitential discipline of the orthodox Church. " How far," he was asked, " does your theory agree with that of Rome ? " " Our theory," he said, " is substantially the same as that of Rome— but," and here a genial smile overspread his face, " our priests are very good-natured." It is the story of a great part of historic religion—the story of a great claim nullified by the practice of those who make it. But in Rome, at least among many priests, this claim to discipline the individual is taken seriously, and the confessional is a part of living religion.

A prominent American layman once attended a mission at the Church of the Paulist Fathers in New York City. He was amazed at what he saw. At five o'clock in the morning, while the city was still dark, the church was crowded with men. " Why can we not do this," he asked, " in our Protestant Churches ? " The answer is simple. Give the minister the power the priest claims and persuade the people that he really possesses it, and you can crowd your churches with worshippers at any hour. For the power that filled that church was the power of the confessional, and the power of the confessional is the power to remit or to reduce the temporal

penalty of sin, both in this life and in that which
is to come.[1]

I am well aware that this power, as defined
by Catholic theologians, is confined within exact
limits, and is not open to the attacks often
made against it by ignorant Protestant con-
troversialists. It is not the power to forgive
sins. That belongs to God alone. Still less is
it the power to permit sin. It is the power,
after appropriate confession and repentance, to
remit a part or all of the temporal punishment
of sin, by substituting a less disagreeable equiv-
alent. Catholic theology distinguishes a double
penalty for sin :—the eternal penalty, which is
the loss of the soul ; the temporal penalty through
which the soul is purified either in this life, or
in purgatory. The latter consists of suffering,
both of body and mind, and may include every
torment which can be conceived by the imagination. God alone can remit the eternal penalty
of sin. But the Church has had committed to
it the power of dispensing with its temporal
punishment. When one reads the lurid pages
of Dante's *Purgatorio* and realizes that what is
there described is believed by multitudes of
Catholics to be actually happening to countless
human beings, among whom their friends or
relatives may be included ; when, on the other

[1] I do not overlook the fact that the disciplinary function
of the Confessional is only one phase of its influence. To many
who use it, it supplies a felt need for direction and counsel, of
which they would gladly avail themselves even if the practice
of confession were not required.

regular performance of the ritual of religion, including in this a number of acts of worship and devotion which have no immediate connection with the formal services of the Church ; in part they consist of acts of kindliness and good-will to one's fellow-men. Charity has in the past played a great rôle in Catholic piety, and the giving of alms has been regarded as a good work in itself, irrespective of its effect upon the recipient. Catholics have planted their hospitals and their orphanages all over the world, but in the main they have confined their ministry either to their own members or to those whom they hoped to win for the Church. Recently, however, Catholic ethics has been giving more attention to man's wider social relationships, and the economic and political questions raised by modern industry are being carefully studied by Catholic scholars. The conservative attitude taken by earlier Catholic pronouncements toward the existing social order is giving place to a more sympathetic and discriminating judgment.[1] So much is this the case that a certain journalist in the United States, whose interest in the current news is more in evidence than his knowledge of history, has prophesied that it would be the Catholic rather than the Protestant Church which would become the champion of the masses, and the foremost leader in the reform of the present social system.

---

[1] Intelligent Roman Catholics frequently date the beginning of this change from the well-known Encyclical of Leo XIII., *Rerum Novarum*, 1891.

How far this will prove to be the case, the future must reveal. But those who entertain rosy hopes of this kind will do well to remember that the test by which the Church judges all good works, whether in the ceremonial or the ethical sphere, is that they must be such as it prescribes and such as will enhance its power. If it must choose between the ceremonial and the ethical side of religion, the ceremonial will come first. This does not mean that the performance of ceremonial acts alone is sufficient apart from inward sincerity, but that a man's attitude towards the ordinances of the Church will be the surest test of his spiritual state. However often and however far a man may fall below the Church's ethical requirements, if he retains his connection with the Church and continues his attendance upon the Sacrament, he has access to a divine resource not available for other men. But if he breaks with the Church he throws this help away.[1]

To be faithful in the performance of one's religious duties, then, and to deal justly and kindly with one's neighbour is to fulfil Rome's ethical requirement for the ordinary Christian. But for the exceptional spirit the Church has something at once more exacting and more rewarding. It summons him to the great task of

[1] This was the excuse given by a Roman Catholic priest to a friend of mine, a neighbouring Protestant minister, for failing to discipline one of his parishioners who was responsible for maintaining a particularly demoralizing saloon which was corrupting the boys of the community.

6

winning for the Church the entire world. For him service becomes propaganda.

This lies in the genius of imperialistic religion. To one who holds the Catholic faith, there can be no service comparable to winning one's fellow-men to the allegiance of Mother Church. The more intelligent one is, the more clearly one will see this; the more unselfish he is, the more keenly he will feel it. When, after long wandering, Newman found his way to Rome at last, it was, he says, like coming into port after long tossing on the open sea. A generous spirit would sacrifice all that he has to share such a gift with others. And could he scruple at any step necessary to make such sharing possible?

It is only against this background that we can understand the ethics of the Roman Catholic propaganda. It is the ethics of militant imperialism everywhere—the ethics of war, not of peace, though for the Roman, as for most other imperialists, the ultimate goal is a peace that shall know no end. This consciousness of a divine commission to dominate at all costs explains the puzzling and unlovely features of Catholic apologetic, its lack of frankness, its willingness to yield all for the one thing necessary. This explains, too, the ruthless attitude toward irre-concilable opponents—the index, the inquisition, and the stake. This explains finally the elaborate machinery through which missionaries are trained and marshalled—the Congregation of the Propaganda and the Society of Jesus. They

are the tools which Rome uses in pursuit of its
one supreme end, the world-wide triumph of
that Church whose victory is identified with the
will of God.

5. *Other Examples of Imperialistic Religion. The Religion of the State and of the Militant Sect*

We have tried as fairly and objectively as we
could to picture imperialistic religion as it is
illustrated in the greatest of its examples—the
Church of Rome. But it is the type we are
primarily interested in, not this particular
example of it. The example we have been
studying is a form of churchly religion. It
identifies submission to the organized Church
with the doing of God's will. But this is by no
means the only illustration we might have
chosen. Besides its churchly form, imperialism
has at least two other forms which have played
a great rôle in history, the religion of the State,
and the religion of the militant sect.[1] The first
—the religion of the State—teaches men to see
in the triumph of the State the fulfilment of
God's purpose, and in submission to the State
the doing of God's will. The second—the religion of the sect—identifies God's will with a
definite set of tenets embodied in a Bible

[1] On the points in which sectarianism differs from the more
consistent forms of imperialism, cf. chap. iv. pp. 125-129. It
will there be shown that sectarianism is a compromise between
individualism and imperialism.

we are not identifying the German people as a whole with this particular type of mentality, any more than we would assert that all Roman Catholics are imperialists in the character of their religious life. The Germany of the Kaiser and the imperial General Staff is not some strange portent revealing the fact that the Germans belong to a different race of beings from other men, and must therefore be permanently ostracized from the society of their fellows, but is only a new illustration of the fact that like causes produce like results, and that if you treat men who call themselves Protestants in the imperialistic way for a long enough time you will get the kind of result the Catholic gets.

But we must not suppose that Germany has any monopoly of the imperialistic spirit in religion. This spirit is found in many men whose political philosophy stands at the opposite pole from hers.[1] Revolutionary Socialism is a striking

[1] Rousseau was an uncompromising opponent of the autocracy of his day, but he has this to say of the demands which the new democratic State which he would substitute may rightfully make upon its citizens. "There is a purely civil profession of faith of which the Sovereign should fix the articles, not exactly as religious dogmas, but as social sentiments without which a man cannot be a good citizen or a faithful subject. While it can compel no one to believe them, it can banish from the State whoever does not believe them,—it can banish him not for impiety, but as an anti-social being, incapable of truly loving the laws and justice, and of sacrificing at need his life to his duty. If any one after publicly recognizing these dogmas behaves as if he did not believe them, let him be punished by death ; he has committed the worst of all crimes, that of lying to the law." *Social Contract*, Eng. trans., New York, 1913, p. 121.

example of imperialistic religion and maintains its hold by an appeal to the same combination of motives. More than one Protestant sect owes its success to similar influences, and could not exist were it not for the desire in men to rule and to be ruled. A recent striking illustration is the militant premillenarianism which has recently been sweeping over wide sections of the United States, attacking the orthodoxy of those who do not accept its tenets and trying to extend its control to the foreign field as well. The spirit of Rome, expelled in theory, still lives on in groups that would most indignantly repel any such association.

Imperialism, we repeat, is the monopoly of no age or social group. Rome is what it is, and has done what it has done, because there is something in men to which imperialism appeals. Till we perceive this we shall not have learned our lesson, nor have understood the world in which we are living.

6. *Motives to which Imperialistic Religion appeals. Its Provision for Men of Other Types. Inconsistency of its Representatives*

What, then, is this " something in man " to which imperialistic religion appeals ? It is not simple but complex, and its emphasis varies from time to time and from person to person. In a recent address Mr. John Drinkwater declared that all the people who really matter in

form of a series of choices to use the means which
the Church provides to ensure the soul's salvation ; for the saint a shorter, if a more arduous,
way is opened in the mystical experience. In
these and similar ways Rome holds to its allegiance
many whose strong individuality no one can
deny.

Even in the realm of thought, where its
censorship is strictest, Rome provides some scope
for the freedom of the individual. When it
comes to matters of faith and morals, there can
be but a single spokesman, and all good Catholics
will yield him implicit obedience. But even when
the Pope speaks *ex cathedra*, he does not speak
out of a vacuum. He acts as interpreter of the
tradition of the past, and that tradition has been
built up gradually through the co-operation of
many minds, and is still in the making. In its
shaping each Catholic scholar may hope to share.
And even when the Church has spoken, and the
limits of free inquiry have been defined, there
remains always the question what the decision
means. Newman in his *Apologia* has reminded
us of the large place which Catholic theory
leaves open to private judgment.[1] The doctrine
of papal infallibility opens new possibilities of
adjustment. This doctrine has often been
attacked as binding the Church to the decisions
of the past, but it may equally be regarded as
a means of emancipation from the tyranny of
history. In his interpretation of tradition, the

[1] *Op. cit.* p. 252.

Pope may bring out some fresh aspect of an
old truth which will, in fact, be a new departure.
In preparing the way for such a reinterpreta-
tion, the inquiring spirit may find scope. The
Modernist movement is an interesting illustration of the attitude I have in mind. As a loyal
son of the Church the Modernist accepts his
condemnation for to-day. But in his heart of
hearts he may still hope that some later pronouncement will prove him in the right after
all, and the supposed heresy of yesterday become
the orthodoxy of to-morrow.[1]

Similar concessions to the spirit of independence are made in other forms of imperialistic
religion. Modern Imperial Germany offers an
instructive example of such accommodation.
In art, in administration, in scholarship, the
individual was given widest scope for his self-
expression. But there were limits which could
not safely be passed. Theologians might be as
critical as they pleased of the Church, past and
present, but to attack the State would be to
run counter to deep-seated religious convictions.
Even Ritschl, most independent of all German
theologians of his generation, taught that the
principles of Christian morality which govern
the conduct of the individual do not apply to
the State.[2]

[1] This is possible because the condemnation of a view does
not necessarily mean that it is false. It may mean only that
it is misleading, or dangerous.

[2] Cf. *Unterricht in der Christlichen Religion* (1875), Eng.
trans., New York, 1901, p. 246.

ism is not simply a stage in the history of religion. It is a recurrent and apparently a permanent religious type. There are men and women whose religious needs, so far as we can see, will always be met in this way. There are tasks to be performed for which a religion of this kind is the most convenient instrument. We may not ourselves like it. We may perceive clearly its limitations and its defects—we may go farther and say, the dangers with which it threatens other and, as we may believe, finer forms of religion. Still here it is, a fact to be reckoned with, a force to be taken into account ; and not in others only, but in ourselves.

But when we have said this, we must go on to say that, great as it is, it can never hope to be the final or highest form of religion. It does too great violence to profound needs in human nature. It follows its great goal in too crude and external a way. It rouses convictions too deep, stirs opposition too sincere ever to hope for complete victory. What these convictions are and what the forms in which they find expression, we shall study in succeeding chapters.

CHAPTER IV

THE INDIVIDUALISTIC PROTEST AGAINST IMPERIALISM

*1. What is meant by Individualistic Religion.
Positive and Negative Individualism*

IN our last chapter we considered imperialism
—a widespread form of social religion which
identifies loyalty to God with complete
submission to some existing institution believed
to be God's spokesman and representative on
earth. We saw that this institution need not
necessarily be a Church. The State may be
regarded as the supreme organ of God's will or
some militant sect. We found that for us the
most striking and instructive example of imperialistic religion was the Church of Rome.
We studied in turn the worship, the education,
the discipline, the service, and the propaganda
of the Roman Catholic Church. We considered
the needs to which it appeals, the satisfaction
which it promises. We saw that it has much to
offer the individual ; that it presents a wide field
for his activity and for his thought. But it
does not go far enough for the more independent
spirits. Sooner or later there comes a break.

A man must choose between submission and self-expression, the sacrifice of himself in the interest of the institution, or the assertion of his own conscience at any cost. When that time comes a new type of religion is born. Such a type we are now to study. We have called it individualistic religion.

It seems as if the title were a misnomer. Individual religions we can understand. But can we speak of individualistic religion? Is not the very genius of individualism that it refuses to conform to type? To the superficial view this seems the case. Yet in spite of all differences which separate one individualist from another we shall find that there are certain psychological attitudes which differentiate them from persons of another type. These common qualities we are now to study. Our description of them will give us our definition of individualistic religion.

By individualistic religion we shall mean a form of religion whose representatives despair of satisfaction through any existing institution, and find solace in immediate communion between the individual soul and God. It is the religion which William James studies in his *Varieties of the Religious Experience*: "the religion of individual men in their solitude, so far as they apprehend themselves to stand in relation to whatever they may consider the divine." The individualist does not desire the intrusion of other personalities into his relation to God. He may use other men as guides to the door of the temple, but he leaves them behind when he enters ; he may find them again when he has withdrawn, but always with a sense of disillusionment, such as the disciples felt when they descended from the Mount of Transfiguration.

What is true of other persons is true also of institutions. To the consistent individualist the claim of the Church to control his personal religious life seems an impertinence. Liberty, not submission, appears to him the genius of true religion. When a man is truest to himself he is most religious. When he is most free from the shackles of tradition, most original and independent, he becomes most conscious of those eternal verities which transcend time and space, and is closest to God.

It is not meant, of course, that the individualist is unconscious of the presence of other personalities, or oblivious of their need of the same kind of first-hand experience of God which he claims for himself. He is often keenly aware of this need, and may feel it his duty to do what he can to satisfy it. But what he does will be something apart from his own personal experience of God. It will be an addendum to that experience, or a consequence of it. It will contribute nothing new and essential. The individualist may even become a missionary, and spend his life rehearsing the story of what God has done for him. But it will be as one who imparts a complete and finished gift, not as one who seeks some new and added light for himself. To be conscious that God cares

7

for others, and to desire to help them to that
knowledge, is to take the first step on the road to
democratic religion.   But of itself it does not
make a man a democrat.   Democratic religion
in the full sense of that term begins when it
first dawns on a man that God may have something to say to him through the *different* thing
He is saying to his neighbour.

Within this broad field of individualistic
religion, two further types may be distinguished.
In the first a man concentrates upon the relation
between his own soul and God, because all other
satisfactions in life have failed him.   In the
second he finds God so satisfying for His own sake
that he has no zest left for other pleasures.   We
may call these respectively negative and positive
individualism.

2. *Individualism as the Religion of Protest.* *Different Forms which this Protest may take*

In Charles Reade's well-known novel, *The
Cloister and the Hearth*, he presents us with an
imperishable picture of individualistic religion.
It is the life-story of Gerard and Margaret, the
father and mother of the great scholar Erasmus.
Though the form in which the author has clothed
the story is that of fiction, the type of religious
experience which he portrays can be verified in
documents whose authenticity no scholar would
dispute.

Gerard was a young Dutch artist, who had

been designed by his parents for the Church.
But though he began his training for the priesthood he did not finish it. A love affair with the
daughter of a neighbour revealed to him that
his vocation was not for the Church, and he
determined to earn his living as an artist, so
as to be able to marry. This did not suit the
plans of his parents, who had small faith in the
artistic abilities of their son, and had no mind to
be saddled with the support of another daughter.
To escape their opposition Gerard marries secretly,
and leaving his bride on their wedding night, sets
out for Italy, where he achieves great success,
and soon finds himself in ample funds. On the
eve of his return he receives a letter from his
brothers telling him that Margaret is dead, and
in the revulsion of feeling he throws prudence
to the winds, and plunges into every form of
dissipation. In this irresponsible state he is
found by a friar who recalls him to himself and
convicts him of his sin. A second change of
feeling follows, as abrupt as the first. He now
interprets the death of his wife as God's punishment for his sin in failing to enter the Church.
To atone for this apostasy, he re-enters the
cloister, and gives himself with all the fervour of
his artistic nature to the ascetic life. The story
culminates on his return to Holland, when he
learns of the deceit practised upon him by his
brothers, sees and recognizes his wife, and in
despair at this new tragedy, flees from the haunts
of men, and establishes himself as a hermit in

a lonely cave, from which he never ventures
out but at night.

Yet even here he is not at peace. By day
he can occupy his thoughts in meditation and
prayer—but at night this resource fails him. He
sees his wife, " her face irradiated with sunshine,
and her eyes gazing upon him with a look of
ineffable tenderness." Awaking with a start,
he interprets his vision as a temptation of the
Evil One. He renews his austerities, " shortens
his sleep, lengthens his prayers, and substitutes
abstinence for temperance." When this does
not avail, he tries " the most famous of all anti-
dotes—the grand febrifuge of the anchorites—
cold water." He finds the deepest part of the
stream that runs by his cell, clears its bottom
of the large stones, makes a hole where he can
stand in water up to his chin, and at the next
approach of the vision, springs from his bed,
and enters the icy water. The cold freezes his
marrow. " I shall die," he cries, " I shall die,
but better this than fire eternal."

At last the wife from whom he has fled finds
him out, and he can no longer conceal from himself
that it is really she who is standing before him
in the flesh. She pleads with him to leave his
cell, not indeed to return to the old relationship—
that his vows have made for ever impossible—
but to become the vicar of a neighbouring parish
and to use his great gifts in bringing consolation
to others. But this appeal he resists as a temptation of the devil. " Unhappy girl," he replies

to the pleading woman, " would you have me
risk my soul and yours for a miserable vicarage ? "
Again he breaks away, and when she seeks to
restrain him, throws her violently on the ground.
When he sees what he has done an impulse of
compassion comes upon him. He stops, turns
toward her a step—then suddenly flings himself
instead into the icy water. " Kill my body,"
he cries, " but save my soul."

Here we have an extreme case of individualistic religion, a case in which the salvation of a
man's own soul is contrasted not only with happiness, but even with usefulness, and the most
intimate and sacred human relationships are
shunned as temptations of the devil.

In this case the impulse to heroic self-
abnegation came from the failure of the subject's
previous plan of life. He turns from the world
to God, because the world cannot give him his
heart's desire. But individualistic religion may
spring from a nobler motive. It may have its
roots in love for others as well as in love of self.
A man may turn his back upon the world in a
spirit of disillusionment, because it does not
answer his dream of a brotherhood of love.
Many a man to-day has been going through
such a disheartening experience. In his boyhood
he responded to the preaching of the social
Gospel. Like the credulous spirits of our Lord's
day, he let himself believe that " the Kingdom of
God was immediately to appear." [1] He threw

---

[1] Luke xix. 11.

himself into the crusade for better homes, better
schools, fairer methods in industry, a more
peaceable adjustment of international disputes.
He called himself socialist, single-taxer, inter-
nationalist.   But steadily the hard facts of life
have forced their way into his paradise, and he
has seen his Utopia dissolve into thin air.   The
conception of God as a Loving Father who cares
for all men and wishes to do them good no longer
seems credible.   If he is to believe in God at all,
it must be in some more intimate and irrefutable
way.   So he turns his back on the prophets of
the new social order.   If God will save his own
soul he will be content.

Or it may be the Church from which the individualist turns in despair.   We have already
seen that the imperialist recognizes the right of
the individual to freedom up to a certain point,
and is prepared to go a considerable distance to
gratify it.   But, however much he may concede,
there comes a point beyond which he cannot go.
When that point is reached there is nothing for
the free spirit to do but to assert its independence,
cost what it may.   Of the two voices, each claiming to be God's, the individualist is never in
doubt which to heed.   When the disciples were
ordered by the chief priests to cease their preaching, Peter's answer was instant : " Whether it be
right in the sight of God to hearken unto you
rather than unto God, judge ye.   But we cannot
but speak the things we saw and heard." [1]   And

[1] Acts iv. 19, 20.

Luther, facing the combined authority of Church and State at Worms, is conscious of no alternative. " Here stand I, God helping me, I can do no other."

The break may come in various ways. It may come through the mind. A man may be asked to believe something which he knows is not true. It may come through the conscience. He may be required to do something which his moral nature disapproves. Or the issue may be joined over some question of taste, or of feeling. Many a sensitive nature in our day has broken with the Church on this ground and become an individualist in his religion. The ritual of the Church does not satisfy his instinct of worship. He finds the services cold and formal. They do not help him to realize the presence of God. Much that is said and done is offensive to him : some things seem sacrilegious. It matters not how the break comes. When the old tie is broken, the individual finds himself alone. And the new situation brings him face to face with God.

The type of religion thus briefly described may be called negative individualism. The driving power is the desire to find refuge from some overmastering evil—either without or more often within. The individualist of this type must escape from his existing environment ; more difficult still, he must escape from his present self. He must be born again.

William James has described this type of religion in masterly fashion in his *Varieties of*

the Religious Experience. In these lectures, as
we have seen, he distinguishes between two
contrasted types of religion. One of these he
calls the religion of healthy-mindedness, the
other the religion of the sick soul. The healthy-
minded Christian is one to whom religion seems
natural and normal, one who grows up into
religion, as he grows up into citizenship or friendship—the type of Christian described by Horace
Bushnell in his well-known book on Christian
Nurture.[1] The sick soul, on the other hand, is
one to whom religion means deliverance. It is
the way of escape from some dreaded evil, of
salvation from some besetting sin. Religion is
here thought of as a device for introducing
harmony into a divided nature. It was William
James who suggested to Harold Begbie the title
of his widely-read book, *Twice-born Men*—the
book in which he tells the story of Old Born-
drunk and other examples of the triumphs of the
Salvation Army revival-room.

This religion of salvation may assume many
forms. The evils from which man needs deliverance are manifold, and the ways in which rescue
comes beyond our power to catalogue. Sickness, sorrow, sin in all its countless and revolting
forms ; even life itself has been felt as an evil
from which man turns to religion for escape.
There is no single outstanding example of individualistic religion which we can take as our
illustration in the same way in which we used

[1] First published in 1847.

the Church of Rome to illustrate imperialism.
Much of the material which claims our attention
is unfamiliar. Much lies altogether outside the
field of the organized Churches. Some of it
could scarcely claim the name "religion" at all.
If we admit it to our category of religion, it can
only be as a sport or freak, one of the members
of that strange collection which excited William
James's pathological interest, and led to the
description of his book by a witty reviewer, as
" Wild Religions I have known." [1]

But whatever the form taken by individualistic religion, it always involves a first-hand
dealing of the soul with God. Its representatives
differ widely in their conception of God and in
their way of approach to Him. But they are all
agreed that each man must approach God for
himself, and judge for himself what God says to
him. The evangelical hears God speaking in the
Bible, the mystic in the silence of his own soul.
But each insists upon the necessity of the
Testimonium Spiritus Sancti, and each finds in

[1] The United States has been a fertile soil for the growing
of these strange forms of individualistic religion, and we are
only now beginning to give them the attention they deserve.
Christian Science is one of the best known of them, with its
variants, faith healing and new thought—now grown so powerful
and so conventional that we are tempted to forget their early
vagaries. But there are many others less known and less
respectable. Miss Mary Austin, in a penetrating essay on
"Religion in America" (*Century Magazine*, August 1922), calls
attention to the creative activity which is expressing itself
through these neglected and often grotesque forms. But into
the wide field she opens we cannot follow her here.

the peace and inner satisfaction which that
witness brings, the final proof that it is God who
has spoken. Beyond this consciousness of God's
presence in his own soul, the consistent individualist does not feel it necessary to go.

3. *Evangelical Protestantism as a form of Negative
   Individualism.   Parallels   in   the   Roman
   Church.   Buddhism as the Extreme Form of
   Negative Individualism*

The most familiar example of the negative
type of individualism, and the most convenient
for our present purpose, is the form which meets
us in evangelical Protestantism. The great boon
desired is forgiveness, and the great evil to be
shunned is sin. God is thought of primarily as
a Judge whose function it is to sit as guardian
of the law. Before His august majesty each soul
must appear to answer for his deeds whether
they be good or evil. In this supreme test no
one of us can assist his brother. Each must
stand naked and alone in the sight of his God.
And since all have sinned and come short of the
glory of God, all alike deserve and will receive
eternal punishment. This punishment includes
suffering of the most dreadful kind for mind and
body, but the suffering is not the worst punishment. More dreadful still is the loss of the
supreme good for which the individual was
designed, the consciousness of being cast out
from " the comfortable presence of God."

In this situation Jesus Christ, God's divine
Son, intervenes with His miraculous deliverance.
He Himself, innocent though He be, takes upon
Him the penalty of our sin, and by a similar
miracle transfers to us the merit of His righteous-
ness. The awe-struck sinner, looking up into
the face of the Judge, sees the frown of offended
justice pass away, and give place to the Father's
smile of forgiveness. The fear which has hitherto
tortured him is replaced by a strange peace.
The weakness which has thus far paralysed him
is succeeded by a sense of buoyancy and power.
He repeats in his own person the experience
described in the New Testament. " Whereas I
was blind, now I see." " I can do all things in
Him that strengtheneth me." [1]

In describing this familiar type of experience
as individualism I am well aware that I am not
doing justice to all the elements in that experience. Evangelical Protestantism, like the Roman
religion against which it was a protest, is a combination of many different elements. Some of
the old imperialism lives on in Protestantism—
more sometimes than we Protestants like to
realize or are willing to confess. Some elements
of the new democratic religion are already present
—not yet fully self-conscious or adequately expressed. But the prevailing emphasis is individualistic. If one were to choose a single word
to express the genius of the older evangelical
Protestantism it would be individualism.

[1] John ix. 25 ; Phil. iv. 13.

In thus concentrating attention upon the relation between the individual soul and God, Protestantism is following an example set by the older Church. We have spoken more than once of the provision made by Rome for the assertion of the responsibility of the individual. The matter of personal salvation offers a notable example. From one point of view salvation may be looked upon as a gift of God through the Church, but from another it is a task to be achieved by the individual in co-operation with the Church. The entire ritual of the Church with its sacraments and its discipline may be described as a series of steps through which the Church conducts the soul in its search for salvation. At no stage is the responsibility of the individual suffered to lapse. The Church promises to do great things for her children ; but whether she will do any one of them, or whether what she does will prove effective, depends in the last analysis upon what the individual does for himself. Unlike the Calvinistic churches, which throw the entire responsibility of salvation on God and deny man any ability to save himself, Rome insists that each man retains the power of freewill unimpaired, and requires him to use it. There is no moment of time when he can say, " Now the battle is over. My soul is safe." To the last there must be struggle and achievement, uncertainty and strain. Through the whole process the individual and the Church are set over against each other, each co-operating in a task which has for its goal the salvation of the individual soul.

Most extreme of all the forms of negative individualism is Buddhism. Here the evil from which deliverance is sought is life itself. Moved with compassion at the spectacle of human misery in its countless forms, the gentle seer of the East searches in vain for a means of deliverance. But each remedy brings him face to face with some new form of the disease—for each leaves a man still the victim of unsatisfied desire. Give him what you will, he will still ask for more. Take from him what you can, some longing will still remain unsubdued. There is but one way to complete and final salvation. Life itself, the mother of desire, must be destroyed. For desire is the source of all our evils—insatiable desire, consumer of that on which it feeds.

It may indeed seem a paradox to cite as an example of individualism a religion which has for its main object the destruction of the individual. But a good case can be made for doing so. This cry for deliverance is itself an affirmation of the value of the human personality. The soul refuses to be satisfied with the common lot. It demands for itself some more enduring comfort —some peace not of this world, which earth can neither give nor take away. For such enduring satisfaction, it is willing to pay any price—even personality itself.

Scholars are not agreed as to the exact meaning of Nirvana—the goal which Buddhism

promises its devotees as their final heaven.
Does it mean literal annihilation ? Or is it
merely the Eastern way of describing in negative
language the indescribable bliss of life with God
described by Christian saints in language as
negative. It is not necessary for our purpose
to decide. Enough to know that in either case
religion involves complete renunciation of the
world, a first-hand dealing of the individual soul
with the supreme reality.

4. *Examples of Positive Individualism.   Mystical
Religion as a Form of Positive Individualism*

But individualistic religion has its positive
as well as its negative aspects.   One may forget
the world, not because the world is sad, but
because one has found a pleasure still more
satisfying.

This positive individualism has assumed many
different forms.   Sometimes it shows itself in
the mere impulse to self-expression—the *joie de
vivre* which is the characteristic of virile and
creative spirits.   There are men who would
rather fight their way to victory than accept
an easy salvation.   One hears this heroic,
struggling, individualistic note in much of our
modern poetry ; in Henley, for example, and
some of his less distinguished imitators.   But
often individualistic religion strikes a less lofty
note.   It finds its satisfaction, not so much in the
struggle, as in the rewards of victory.   To be

the chosen of the gods when so many are passed by, ministers to the sense of pride. Centuries ago the writer of 2 Esdras gave striking expression to this feeling. When the seer, burdened with the sins of the world, pleads the mercy of God as the sole ground of forgiveness, since " if God did not pardon them that were created by His word and blot out the multitude of offences, there would peradventure be very few left out of an innumerable multitude," the angel replies, " The Most High hath made this world for many, but the world to come for few. . . . Be therefore no longer curious how the ungodly shall be punished, but inquire how the righteous shall be saved—they whose the world is and for whom it was created." [1]

Of all the forms of positive individualism the most interesting for our present purpose is mysticism. It is not possible here to enter upon any lengthy discussion of this much debated subject. Mysticism exercises a perennial fascination for scholars, and forms a debating ground where the most contradictory opinions are maintained with equal assurance and enthusiasm. William James regarded the mystical experience as the heart of all vital religion. Other students of religion are equally certain that it is the mortal foe of ethical religion. All that we can hope to do is to point out some simple distinctions which may help to throw light upon such phases of the mystical experience as at present interest us.

[1] vii. 62–70 ; viii. 1 ; ix. 13.

At the outset we must distinguish between mysticism, considered as a distinct type of the religious experience, and the element of immediacy which enters into all vital religion. In all true religion, of whatever kind, whether it be imperialistic, individualistic, or democratic, the soul is conscious of an inner satisfaction which religion interprets as the presence of God. This immediate sense of God's presence is often described as the mystical element in religion. But this use of the term " mystical " is misleading. It would be wiser to use some other word such as " vital " or " first hand," and to restrict the term " mystical " to those exceptional cases in which the consciousness of God's presence reaches so high a degree of vividness that all other objects drop out of the field of contemplation. These moments are often accompanied by a high degree of satisfaction, rising in that of the great saints to ecstasy. But it is not the ecstasy itself which is the mark of the mystic experience, but the felt presence of God.

Within this narrower sphere of the mystical experience two further types can be distinguished. In one case the sense of God's presence comes through the contemplation of his works, as in the glory of the sunset or the sublimity of the mountain ; in the other case through a process of pure abstraction, in which not only the human individual, but even nature itself is dissolved into nothingness. In this most inner and secret shrine, thought itself fails. Only feeling remains,

and this feeling must of necessity remain
voiceless. William James had this aspect of the
mystical experience in mind when he specified
ineffability as one of its four characteristics.[1]
When St. Catharine of Genoa was asked by her
children to describe her experience, she could
not do it. " O would I could tell what my heart
feels. And her children would say, O Mother,
tell us something of it. And she would answer,
I cannot find words appropriate to so great a
love. But this I can say with truth, that if of
what my heart feels but one drop were to fall
into hell, hell itself would altogether turn into
eternal life." [2]

One may question whether the term individualism can rightly be used to describe this
abstract and sublimated form of religion. The
mark of the mystical experience, as described by
many of the great mystics, is that all thought of
the individual is forgotten and the soul loses
itself completely in the contemplation of God.
In many points the manuals of mystical religion
differ, but they all agree that the surest path to
the presence of God is through the suppression
of desire. " *Gelassenheit*," " passivity," " letting
oneself go," are terms which recur again and
again. Another recurring term is inwardness.
There are barriers to be passed behind which the
Deity is hidden, and the self is one of the most

---

[1] *Varieties of the Religious Experience*, p. 380.
[2] Quoted in von Hügel, *The Mystical Element in Religion,
as studied in St. Catharine of Genoa*, i. p. 119.

8

formidable. Not only must the flesh be subdued, but the imagination and the desires must be brought into captivity. Thought itself must cease, the personality become an empty vessel.[1] " O to be nothing, nothing, simply to lie at His feet," is a truthful description of one aspect of the mystical experience.

Yet, in spite of this apparent inconsistency, the use of the term individualism can be defended. The characteristic feature of individualistic religion, as we have defined it, is the exclusion of other individuals from one's most intimate religious experiences. Up to the forecourt one may make one's pilgrimage in company, but the Holy of Holies each must enter alone. St. Theresa has much to tell us here that is illuminating. She realizes that God's choicest gifts are too rare to be enjoyed all the time. Sometimes, she reminds her disciples, it is God's will that we should leave our privacy for a while and resume our homely duties of ministry. Let us accept the sacrifice with a cheerful heart. When the discipline is complete, He will recall us to Himself. But in the meantime the sacrifice remains a sacrifice. Of the two states, the social and the solitary, St. Theresa has no doubt which is the higher.[2]

[1] Cf. *St. John of the Cross: The Ascent of Mount Carmel*, Eng. trans., 1906.

[2] Cf. *The Life of St. Theresa*, Eng. trans. by Dalton, London, 1851, p. 335. " For though I was desirous to separate myself from every one, and to follow my profession and vocation with the greatest perfection and enclosure, yet I desired this in

Experiences of this kind are found in all religions. In Christianity they are common to Protestantism and to Catholicism. But it is in the Roman Catholic Church that the mystical experience has been most fully and most successfully cultivated. Herrmann, in his well-known book, *The Communion of the Christian with God*,[1] argues that mysticism is the typically Catholic form of piety, in contrast to Protestantism, where the conscious relation to Jesus as an individual remains even during the experience of communion with God. Certainly the mystical experience is the last and highest gift which Rome has to offer to the individual in search of vital religion. It is Rome's proudest boast that she produces saints. The saint has a more intimate experience of God than others, and need not be bound by the rules prescribed for the guidance of less favoured mortals. He may be trusted to

such a way that whenever I understood it would tend more to God's honour to abandon all this, I would have done it with tranquillity and cheerfulness, as I did before." Cf. p. 339: " I went home thinking they would put me in prison. This, I thought, would be a great comfort to me, for then I should not speak to any one, and would be able to repose a little while in solitude ; and this was necessary to me, for by conversing so often with people, I became, as it were, ground to the dust." Speaking of the sisters of the new and stricter convent which she had founded at Avila, she says (p. 346): " Their whole study is to know how to advance further in the service of God. Solitude is their delight, and the very thought of any one, even if it should be one of their nearest relatives, is a great affliction to them, unless they hope to be able to excite such persons to renewed love for their spouse."

[1] Eng. trans., London, 1895.

do nothing which will impugn the authority of
the Church, or diminish her prestige ; but with
this proviso, he is left free to follow God's leading
wherever he will.   The great mystics, whom we
have characterized as typical individualists, were
many of them nurtured in the bosom of the
Catholic Church, and remained to their death
her loyal children.   Yet the centre of their interest
was not in the Church, but in the piety her
shelter and protection made possible.   In the
Church, they were not of the Church, though the
Church claimed them for her own, and gloried
in their achievements.   That Rome has been
able to make place within her fold for such
thoroughgoing   individualists   is   the   supreme
example of her skill as a ruler of men's spirits.

5. *The Puritan Combination of Positive and Negative Individualism*

Such, then, are the two main types of individualistic religion—the negative type which
finds expression in evangelicalism, and the positive
which is illustrated in mysticism.   Sometimes
the two combine in interesting ways, as in that
great seer, Jonathan Edwards, who made the
legalistic Calvinism of his day the vehicle of a
mystical piety.   Edwards, in this a true mystic,
found the heart of religion in the vision of God.
But Edwards saw the God of Calvinism, with his
dual decree and his divided universe.   Calvin
looked on the dark side of the picture, and turned

his face away. For what he saw, he could find
no reason but the inscrutable will of God. But
Edwards gazes into hell and sees its fires trans-
figured with a strange and awful beauty. Hell is
the way in which God's justice is manifested, and
if for this countless individuals must perish, that
is the price that must be paid for the raptures of
the rest. Only as an expression of this mystic
ecstasy—the joy in the terrible which closes the
mouth of Job when God appears in the storm,
can we understand Edwards' words in that sermon
which remains the most startling *tour de force*
of individualistic religion : " The end of the
world contemplated by the righteous ; or the
torments of the wicked in hell, no occasion of
grief to the saints in heaven." [1]

" You that have godly parents, who in this
world have tenderly loved you, who were wont
to look upon your welfare as their own, and were
wont to be grieved for you when anything cala-
mitous befell you in this world, and especially
were greatly concerned for the good of your
souls, industriously sought and earnestly prayed
for your salvation, how will you bear to see them
. . . now without any love to you, approving
the sentence of condemnation, when Christ shall
with indignation bid you depart, wretched,
cursed creatures into eternal burning ? How
will you bear to see and hear them praising the
Judge for His justice exercised in pronouncing
this sentence, and hearing it with holy joy in their

[1] Sermon XIII. (*Works*, New York, 1869, vol. iv. pp. 296,
297).

countenances, and shouting forth the praises and hallelujahs of God and Christ on that account ? You that have godly husbands or wives or brethren or sisters with whom you have been wont to dwell under the same roof, and to eat at the same table, consider how it will be with you when you shall come to part with them, when they shall be taken and you left. . . . However you may wail and lament when you see them parted from you . . . you will see in them no signs of sorrow that you are not taken with them."

This seems the last word in unquestioning submission. Yet some of our Puritan Fathers achieved something even more incredible. They were willing, if need be, themselves to be damned for the glory of God.[1]

6. The Monastery and the Sect as Social Expressions of Individualistic Religion

Thus far we have been describing individualistic religion considered as a personal experience, a protest against other forms of social religion or a substitute for them. But even in the most extreme form of individualistic religion complete isolation proves impossible. The hermit may flee to the desert, but his solitude will not long remain unbroken. Sooner or later others will

[1] A similar combination of negative and positive individualism meets us in the Buddhist conception of Nirvana as the supreme goal of humanity.

follow him. In religion as in every other realm
of life some form of association proves inevitable.
Even Gerard could not maintain himself alone.
The cell he occupied, another hermit had digged,
and the food he ate was brought to him by his
neighbours. It is not a question of like or dis-
like, but of sheer necessity. If it be only for
self-preservation there must be some kind of
association. The question is not whether the
individualist will have social institutions, but
what kind of institutions they will be.

Two possibilities are open to him. He may
be content with the minimum of organization,
just enough to keep life going and to ensure the
platform on which his own feet can safely stand.
Or he may be convinced that his own type of
experience is one which God means that he
should share with others, and for that reason
feel it his duty to create an organization for the
purpose of propagating it. In the first place
his Church will be a community—monastic or
otherwise ; in the second case it will be a sect.

The most natural institutional expression of
individualistic religion is the independent and
self-centred community. Such a community
may differ widely in detail. Its members may
practise the celibate life, or they may include
families of like-minded persons—but whether
celibate or married, they will not be interested
in propaganda. They will be content to live
their own lives in their own way, and guard the
liberty so hardly won. If others come to join

them, it is their affair. The Brothers will not repel newcomers, but neither will they encourage them. They have another and a higher aim, to cultivate their own souls and to enjoy the peace of God which passeth understanding.

The typical example is the monastery. Here the devotees of the solitary life combine to protect their own privacy. Each has his cell to which he can retire,[1] and while they meet for common worship and for the work necessary to sustain life, these are incidents in the main purpose which brings them together, which is solitude. In extreme cases, as with the Trappists, even speech is forbidden.

It is of course true that other factors have been operative in the history of monasticism, besides the desire to promote the individual religious life. The founders of the great orders were well aware that man has many needs, and that if they were to maintain a sane and healthy life they must make provision for work and study as well as for prayer. Monasticism, as developed by a genius like Benedict of Nursia and his successors, proved a great civilizing agency. The monks became farmers, scholars, teachers. But the ideal remained individualistic. Central in the life of each brother were the hours spent alone with God, and the social contacts with people outside the brotherhood were inci-

---

[1] This is true, to be sure, only of the stricter orders—those which make contemplation the sole object of the monk's life. In many monasteries, common or dormitory life was the rule.

dents in an experience which in the last analysis
was independent of anything they could give.
When prosperity brought laxity, as it was sure
to do, the first step in reform was a renewed
insistence upon a life of immediate communion
with God, and the recovery of the lost hours of
devotion.

But individualistic religion may take another
course. The insight that comes in solitude may
seem too precious to be monopolized. The
impulse to fellowship which is latent in every
man may begin to assert itself. When this
moment comes a new social interest begins to
operate. A purely self-centred and isolated life
seems no longer adequate. There must be an
active and aggressive organization. The community must add to contemplation, propaganda.

This development may be studied both in
Catholicism and in Protestantism. The orders
which came into existence for the purpose of
providing a way of escape from the world, not
to say from the Church, proved useful agencies
in subduing the world to the Church. New orders
were founded whose primary purpose was to
spread the true religion. St. Francis and St.
Dominic made preaching central in their programme. Ignatius Loyola gave the hierarchy its
most effective weapon for combating the reform-
ing spirit of the sixteenth century. In the
Society of Jesus we see a militant monasticism,
using the methods of individualistic religion to
discipline soldiers for the battles of imperialism.

Somewhat similar was the development of individualistic religion in Protestantism. When Luther broke with Rome, the last thing he expected to do was to found a new Church. He had but one concern, which was to save his soul. But he soon found that others were to be considered as well as himself. He was not the only one who had passed through a revolutionary experience. These other seekers after God turned to him for help and guidance. Little by little he was forced into a position of leadership. The solitary became a reformer; the reformer, the founder of a Church.

The experience of Luther repeated itself in the case of other Protestants. Many of the great denominations began as little societies for the cultivation of personal religion. Only gradually did expanding numbers alter the perspective, and transform them into Churches. A notable example is Methodism, one of the most numerous and most powerful of all the Protestant families, which, as is well known, began as a little group of societies for the self-discipline of their members.

In the new Churches, to be sure, the old individualistic ideal was still controlling. All that was done was designed to make the individual vividly conscious of his immediate relationship to God. This was true of the use made of the Bible. Perfect and inerrant as it was in all its parts, the Bible remained a sealed book, unless its meaning was opened to the reader by the Spirit. The authority of Protestantism is not

the Bible alone, but the Spirit of God bearing
witness to the heart and conscience of the believer
that this book is God's word to him.[1]

This conception of religious authority has its
consequences for education.   True education must
fit a man to see with his own eyes and make
his own ultimate decisions. Conversion—the
deliberate act of the will by which a man re-
nounces sin and embraces God—plays a great
rôle in individualistic religion.   But it is only
the first step in a training which is lifelong.   At
each stage in this training individual responsibility is emphasized.   Each man must read the
Bible for himself, and make his own independent
decisions on the basis of what he reads.   Each
must pray his own prayer, and expect his own
answer. With each God deals at first hand.
No one's experience can take the place of his
neighbour's.

The public worship of the Church is planned
to assist this process of self-education.   The
worshipper is bidden to forget the world and its
cares ; to concentrate his thought upon the soul
and its destiny.   He is introduced into the society
of those who have found salvation before him,
but only as a step towards that more intimate
communion with God in which all other individuals are forgotten.

Central in the entire process of education is
the discipline of the will.   There are rules to be
followed ; renunciations to be made.   These are

[1] *Westminster Confession*, chapter i.

concerned with such matters as Bible reading
and prayer, Sabbath observance and temperance,
as well as the homely virtues of honesty and
charity.   They vary in their details in the different
Churches, but they agree in this, that the discipline is in the last analysis self-discipline.   Others
may help in the initial stages, but unless the
believer becomes captain of his own soul his
education will have failed of its purpose.

The ideal of service is conceived in similar
individualistic fashion.   We serve our neighbour,
explains Luther in his discussion of Christian
freedom, in order to show our gratitude to God for
what He has done for us.   And the best thing that
we can do for some one else is to bring him where
he will see God for himself.   The ordinary civic
virtues are, to be sure, important—honesty,
charity, justice, and the like.   God requires
these of His children, and Protestant Christianity
has made notable contributions to social ethics,[1]
but for the Christian the supreme duty is witness.
There is only one effective way to bring others
to Christ, and that is to tell them what God has
done for us.   Personal testimony is central in
the propaganda of Protestantism, and the re-
vival room wins its converts by the contagion of
personal experience.

It is when service takes the form of propaganda that the individualist faces for the first
time, in its full force, the social problem which
is central for the imperialist and the democrat.

[1] Cf. the monograph of Troeltsch, already cited.

Two possibilities are open to him. He may trust his neighbour so far only as his neighbour's main conclusions agree with his own ; or he may be consistent in his individualism and leave his neighbour free to make his own decision, even though that decision be one he himself disapproves. To take the first course is to follow a path which will lead back sooner or later to imperialism. To follow the second is to take the first step on the road to democratic religion.

7. *The Sectarian Compromise between Individualism and Imperialism*

We may follow Troeltsch in using the term " sect " to describe the new form of religious institution which results when the first path is taken. The religion of the sect is individualistic religion which has carried over into its new environment the imperialistic spirit. The sectarian is an individualist in his own personal religious experience. He hears God speaking to him directly, and implicitly obeys. But he believes that God must say the same thing to every other man. He cannot tolerate the thought of any variation in religion. As with the imperialist his goal is conformity. Yet his philosophy will not permit him to create the institutions through which the imperialist achieves complete conformity. So he is obliged to seek the same goal by an indirect road. In theory each man is free to approach God for himself, and to interpret what he finds in his own way. But in practice any departure from the accepted interpretation is regarded as dangerous,—all the more dangerous because it is presented in the guise of personal experience. Indeed it may be said that heresy is even more disturbing to the sectarian than to the consistent imperialist, for it poisons the wells of which he drinks. In the name of freedom of conscience the Nonconformist sets up again the methods of social control, to escape from which he himself broke with the Church.

In choosing the term " sect " to designate the second form in which individualism finds institutional expression, we do not use the word in any derogatory sense, but simply as a convenient designation of a clearly recognizable religious type. In imperialistic religion, the institution is the bond of union, and within the limits it permits, variety both of opinion and conduct is permissible, even praiseworthy. In sectarian religion, on the other hand, a particular set of tenets is identified with absolute truth, and those only who accept them are eligible to membership. One may be born into the Church. One must join a sect. In practice, therefore, sectarian religion is commonly divisive. It lacks the power of adaptation which is possessed by the more consistent forms of imperialism. Troeltsch has much to say of the provincial character of sectarianism.[1] He finds its genius

---

[1] *Op. cit.* p. 362.

best illustrated in the more radical groups of the later Middle Ages. By contrast the larger bodies which came into existence as the result of the Protestant Reformation are to be understood as examples of churchly religion.

This way of describing the difference, however, fails to do justice to the sectarian element in the older Protestantism. What differentiates sectarian religion from thoroughgoing imperialism is not that one is an example of churchly religion and the other is not, but that the sectarian makes every religious person responsible for determining the marks which the true Church should possess, whereas the imperialist denies him that responsibility. In the one case private judgment is an essential function of the individual Church member ; in the other it is not. But the sectarian may be just as conscious as any other Churchman that his Church possesses absolute truth, and that it is his duty to make all other persons acknowledge this.

In the early days of Protestantism we find many instances of this combination of individual responsibility with intolerance toward others. When Luther broke with Zwingli on the interpretation of the Lord's Supper, and took his stand on his own understanding of the words " *Hoc est corpus meum*," he was a true sectarian. The same was true of the Calvinists at the Synod of Dort, when they read the Arminians out of the Church because they could not accept the Calvinistic interpretation of the divine decree.

Yet both Lutherans and Calvinists claimed to speak in the name of the Church universal, and believed themselves to be maintaining the continuity of the Christian tradition. We to-day see the inconsistency of their action and are able to account for it historically. But at the time it seemed the only course possible if they were to be true both to conscience and Church.

In our own day the sectarian spirit is a factor to be reckoned with in our efforts to realize Christian unity. It will help us to deal with it intelligently if we think of it as one of the natural ways in which individualistic religion expresses itself. We must not let the varieties of its manifestation blind us to the essential unity of the type. At first sight there seems nothing in common between the Anglo-Catholic, with his profound reverence for antiquity and his insistence upon the necessity of the three orders of the ministry, and the American Southern Baptist who makes the local congregation the final seat of ecclesiastical authority and requires immersion as a pre-requisite to communion. But it would help each to understand the other if they could realize that they are both alike examples of sectarian religion in the technical sense. Both make a particular interpretation of Christianity not shared by many of their fellow-Christians, even Christians of their own communion, their test of other men's orthodoxy, and their reason for granting or refusing them fellowship. The fact that the Anglo-Catholic claims to do this in

the name of the Church, and the Baptist on the
authority of the Bible, does not alter the significance of what they are doing in the least. At
heart they are both individualists, and make
their own conviction the norm of the Church
universal.

We must not confuse sectarianism as thus
defined with what is known to-day as denominationalism. Sectarianism describes an attitude
of mind. Denominationalism calls attention to
a method of organization. Under the denominational system we find many bodies of Christians
living side by side and co-operating in many
ways for Christian purposes. Denominationalism
may be ineffective as a method of Church government, but in its tolerant spirit it is an expression
of democratic religion, whereas sectarianism perpetuates the imperialistic spirit in Protestantism.
The democrat may criticize denominationalism,
but he can live with it, and hope to improve it.
Sectarianism and democracy are a contradiction
in terms.

8. *Strength and Weakness of Individualistic Religion. Its Psychological Basis, and its
Social Significance*

Such in brief description is individualistic
religion, with its sharp contrasts and its everchanging history. What place shall we give it
in our estimate of religious values ?

There are three possible angles from which

9

we may judge individualistic religion. We may think of it as a protest against imperialism. We may regard it as an independent and permanent religious type. We may see in it the forerunner of democratic religion.

As a protest against imperialistic religion, individualism is abundantly justified. Again and again when things were darkest, both in Church and State, brave spirits have dared to break with existing authority in the interest of a larger freedom. Jesus Himself was crucified because He would not conform. Without the heroes and martyrs of individualism not one of all our priceless liberties would have been won, and the freedom which is now possible within Church and State alike would not be ours. In a different sense from that in which it is ordinarily understood, the blood of the martyrs has been the seed of the Church. That so many conscientious men and women find it possible to live a satisfying life both in Church and State to-day is due to the fact that many others have dared to leave the Church, and to defy the State.

As an independent type of religion, too, there is much to be said for individualism. There are persons whose conscience drives them into the wilderness. They must meet God in solitude if they are to find Him at all. We must make a place in our social theory for these restless and adventurous souls. Pioneers of the spirit, like Kipling's Explorer, they push their way into regions which but for them would have remained undiscovered. But where they have gone others will follow. The visions seen by them in solitude become the commonplaces of a later age. The example they set in their loneliness is followed by others who do not need to make their sacrifices. We have seen in the Roman Catholic orders a conspicuous example of the social uses of the solitary life. Coming into existence in the first instance to protect the seclusion of their members, they have become social agencies of high civilizing value. A similar experience repeats itself in Protestantism. Above all other Protestant Christians the Friends have insisted that the individual must be silent before his God. But what God has said to them in their solitude they have lived out in the sight of men.

The psychological basis of individualistic religion is the self-regarding impulse in man. There is something in each one of us which desires expression ; something in which we feel ourselves different from our neighbours. We are independent personalities with needs and rights of our own. This sense is developed in varying degrees in different individuals. Often it takes unlovely and even dangerous forms. But when it is lacking altogether we feel that something fundamentally human is absent. A man who does not value himself will not be respected by others. A man who has not the courage to resist what his conscience condemns is morally defective. Even altruism would be impossible without the

self-regarding spirit. Before you can surrender
you must be master. In order that you may
share, you must possess.

A second psychological root of individualistic
religion is the law of rhythm in human life.[1]
It is a fact of experience that if we are to work
well we must rest often ; if we are to live effectively in society we must have our hours alone.
In quiet we not only renew our energies ; we
come to know ourselves. That mysterious realm
of the subconscious of which we hear so much
to-day is with us always, and, whether we wake
or sleep, its register of impressions is ceaselessly
in operation. But we learn what it has to teach
us in the moments when we are alone. Our
great insights, our best inspirations come to us
in solitude. " Be still, and know that I am
God," is good psychology as well as good religion.
But when we take this phase of our life and treat
it as if it were the whole we act unreasonably.
Unbroken solitude may be as demoralizing as
uninterrupted companionship, as the story of
the monks abundantly proves. Even of the great
mystics it is true that, so far as their visions
profess to bring a definite content of knowledge,
that knowledge can be traced to sources which
they owe to contact with their fellow-men. What
is new is the combination of elements, the in-
tensity with which they are appreciated, and the
fresh uses which are made of them. Contempla-

[1] Cf. the suggestive discussion of Professor Hocking in his
Meaning of God in Human Experience, chap. xxviii.

tion and activity are the two poles of the normal
life. We neglect either at our peril.

In individualistic religion, finally, we touch
the creative element in human experience. That
mysterious power of the spirit by which we form
old materials into new combinations and make
out of parts a whole which has meaning and
beauty is in a peculiar sense the prerogative of the
individual. Others may respond to the insight,
when it has been expressed. Others may appropriate the truth when it has been formulated.
The Church may make the prophet's words its
own, and clothe them in the conventional garb
of institutional religion. The fact remains that
the vision came to the prophet when he was alone,
and till appropriated by others remained his
private and personal possession. Indeed we may
go further. In the last analysis institutional
religion itself owes its existence to the creative
insight of the individual. He builds the house
in which his successors live, often long after they
have forgotten who it was that built it.

We must make room in our religion, then, for
the individual, and give him the honour which is
his due. But when he insists upon making his
own type of insight and experience a finality,
he ceases to be a help and becomes a menace.
Either he loses himself in the contemplation of
God and is content to let the world go on its way
without his help, or he makes his own experience
the standard for all. We have seen illustrations
of both tendencies in the older Protestantism.

It carried at its heart an unresolved antinomy.
It boasted of freedom while insisting on uniformity, but the two claims are incompatible.
We may have one or the other. We cannot have
both. Yet Protestantism in its churchly form
has until recently been unwilling to surrender
either. It has been a half-way house between
imperialism and democracy, having broken with
the one without having attained the other.
Now freedom has been emphasized, now uniformity. Sometimes the individualistic spirit
has gained the upper hand, and again the imperialist has had the mastery. In this conflict
there seems no hope either of surrender or of
victory.[1]

But there is another path which may be
followed which promises a happier outcome.
One may carry one's individualism one step
further, and recognize that God may speak to
others in as unique and original a way as He has

[1] Professor Hauter, in the instructive article already quoted,
has given an illuminating account of this inner conflict. Cf.
esp. p. 40: " The sociological problem of Protestantism thus
appears to us under a double aspect. On the one hand,
Protestantism, in principle and in type of worship, tends to
emphasize individual piety, and to weaken, if not destroy,
gregarious religion. On the other hand, gregarious religion is
strongly entrenched in the Protestant Churches. It gives
them their foundation, and effectively counterbalances the
individualistic tendencies, without consciously setting out to do
so. The result is that Protestantism as religious ideal is in strife
with Protestantism as ecclesiastical institution. To put it in
another way, in the measure that Protestantism realizes its
true nature, it destroys the foundation of its existence and of
its historic unity."

spoken to oneself. One may abandon once and for all the ideal of uniformity, and find the key to the free co-operation of individuals in their common experience of an expanding knowledge and an enlarging life. This new creative form of religion has long been slowly forming itself side by side with the older types, but not until recently has it come to full self-consciousness. We have called it democratic religion.

CHAPTER V

DEMOCRATIC RELIGION

1. *What is meant by Democratic Religion*

DEMOCRATIC religion—the third member of our group—cannot be so easily studied as imperialism or individualism. It has not yet found equally consistent expression, either personal or institutional. In the individual it remains largely an aspiration; for the group a programme, not only unachieved, but in part unformulated.

We have described democratic religion provisionally as the type of religion in which the call to comradeship is most clearly heard and in which the thought of others enters as an integral part into one's relation to God. But it is possible to be democratic to a greater or less degree. One may be a democrat in thought but not in conduct, or in feeling but not in thought. One may even be democratic in thought, feeling, and conduct but limit the sense of comradeship to a definite group. Aristocracy, considered as a personal attitude and not as a social distinction based on either rank or wealth, admits of the free spiritual fellowship characteristic of democracy, but confines it to a limited number of persons, more or less rigidly fixed.

Our difficulty is further accentuated by the fact that the democratic spirit has not yet succeeded in creating institutions adequate to its expression. It remains as a leaven in the older organizations, modifying their development to a greater or less degree. Thus denominational Protestantism may be regarded either as a group of rival sects or as an emerging free democracy, according as greater weight is laid upon one or other of its constituent elements. Sabatier, as we have seen, classes the older Protestantism (the religion of the Book) as a religion of authority with Catholicism (the religion of the Church) over against the religion of the Spirit which includes both individualism and democracy; whereas Harnack, laying more stress on the free creative elements in the religion of the Reformers, regards Protestantism as a single type in contrast to both the great historic forms of Catholicism.[1]

---

[1] The fact that Harnack includes under the single category " Protestantism " the rigid individualistic type of religion which we have called Sectarianism, and the freer democratic type which makes room for difference and progress, is no doubt in part to be explained because the difference between these two types is expressed in no difference in outward organization corresponding to the break between the Greek and Roman Churches. Yet Sabatier has shown that we are dealing with types quite as distinct. As Greek Christianity represents the static form of institutionalism, while the Roman Catholic Church in its power of adaptation and adjustment is the typical example of thoroughgoing imperialism, so the older Protest-

We must therefore construct our picture of democratic religion by combining the common elements in many different examples, giving preference to those in which the democratic spirit finds most thoroughgoing and consistent expression.

Thirty odd years ago a young English physician faced the question of his life's future. He had completed his professional studies with distinction, and was looking about for a practice, when a friend happened to call his attention to the condition of the deep sea fishermen in the North Sea. It seems that some good people, moved by the loneliness and exposure of these fishers' lives, and, above all, by their almost complete deprivation of the conventional forms of religion, had conceived the plan of fitting out a little steamer to accompany them on their fishing trips as a floating chapel and house of friendship. The boat was secured, equipped and manned, with a single exception. A surgeon was needed who would be willing to make the steamer his headquarters and practise his profession among the fishermen, while at sea.

The idea appealed to the young doctor's

antism represents the first of the two alternative forms which individualistic religion of the missionary kind may take—the rigid, uncompromising type we have called sectarianism — whereas the later Protestantism has adopted the other possible alternative, and is becoming more and more consistently democratic. Cf. my article, " Is our Protestantism still Protestant ? " *Harvard Theological Review*, 1908, p. 28 seq.

spirit of adventure. He abandoned the thought
of a conventional practice, applied for the post,
and became the physician of the London Deep
Sea Mission.

Some years later a second call came to him,
which carried him to a new continent. Hard as
is the lot of the North Sea fishermen of England,
their time at sea comes to an end at last, and
when they turn their faces homeward, they
reach a country where there are churches and
schools, hospitals and libraries, and all the other
accompaniments of a Christian civilization. But
there were other fisher-folk of the same stock
who are not so fortunate. Along the North-
east shore of British America there stretches the
lonely coast known as the Labrador. Here live
the Canadian fishermen, who ply their trade in
the North Atlantic. These had no schools, no
hospitals, few churches—only the saloon and
the trader's store. Men died for want of a
doctor. Minds starved for lack of a teacher.
Souls with deep religious longings were left
unshepherded, because their fellow-Christians
had forgotten them.

The thought of these lonely people would not
let the young doctor alone. If no one else was
available he determined to go to them. So he
bade good-bye to his friends in the North Sea,
and started on this new adventure.

What Wilfred Grenfell has done in thirty
years in the Labrador is too well known to
need retelling. Hospitals have been established,

staffed and sustained. Industries have been
started, schools provided, churches enlarged and
strengthened. The conscience of two continents
has been aroused, and friends raised up by the
thousand who have made these lonely lives their
concern. But what interests us here is what
has been going on in Grenfell himself. If you
asked him what first took him to the Labrador
he would tell you, " Religion." If you asked
him what the Labrador had given him in return,
he would still answer, " Religion."

In his journey from one hospital to another
along the coast, it was often necessary for Dr.
Grenfell, when navigation was no longer possible,
to traverse some inlet of the sea on the ice. On
one of these journeys a sudden change of the
weather cut him off from the mainland and set
him adrift on an ice-pan which was carrying him
out to the open sea. Like Gerard, he found
himself alone in bitter cold. But whereas the
individualist Gerard risked death as a means
of saving his own soul, Grenfell the democrat
could think only of how his death might affect
the work he was engaged in. " Except for
my friends," he writes, " I had nothing I could
think of to regret whatever." [1] When, after
hours of exposure, deliverance came at last, he
was glad to be back once more with a new lease
of life before him. " I had learned on the pan
many things, but chiefly that the one cause for
regret, when we look back on a life which we

[1] Grenfell, *A Voyage on a Pan of Ice*, Boston, 1908, p. 10.

think is closed for ever, will be the fact that we have wasted its opportunities." [1]

A type of religion is illustrated in this life-story which is clearly distinguishable from the others we have observed. The responsibility of the individual is one of its fundamental beliefs. The missionary spirit is its moving force. But its characteristic note is fellowship. The democrat in religion trusts men and is trusted by them. Wherever man meets man, he finds God at work. Dr. Post, of the Syrian Protestant College in Beirût, was able to enter sympathetically into the prayer life of the devout Mohammedans with whom his work as a surgeon brought him into contact, and to detect, beneath the differences in form, a common piety. Dr. Timothy Richard of Shanghai won the confidence of his Chinese neighbours so completely that they even allowed him to interpret their religion to others. At a congress of religions when stage fright overtook

---

[1] *Ibid.* p. 14. In a later article, he explains more fully what these opportunities were. " Over thirty years in the North has left me an increasingly confirmed belief in the worthful-ness of the people, who by their simplicity, rugged honesty, and latent ability, more than justify any effort made on their behalf, by the return they make to the world, and the contribution they will yet make to the future. My own association with them, over a period of many years and in time of stress, as well as when life's outlook was brightest for them, has been a source of infinite satisfaction to me. Those who know them most intimately would agree with me that we are in the debt of those men, and that the North has been able to give back to us ten times what we have been able to offer to it " (" Thirty Years in the Labrador," *Congregational Quarterly*, London, April 1923).

the Taoist Pope, he turned to Dr. Richards and said, " Will you speak for me ? " and the Christian missionary gave a sympathetic presentation of Taoism to the audience. The sympathy of Miss Jane Addams with the men and women of many nationalities living in the neighbourhood of Hull House brought a new realization of the meaning of Christian brotherhood first to a great city, and then to the whole nation. In these and similar experiences we are aware of a new approach to God. They are examples of democratic religion.

2. *Democratic Religion distinguished from the Religion of Equality ; from the Religion of the Majority. The Place of Progress in Democratic Religion*

In choosing the name " democratic " to describe the religion of fellowship, we must guard ourselves against a natural misconception. To many readers the term " democracy " has an exclusively political connotation. Dean Inge, in his *Outspoken Essays,*[1] has warned us of the danger of an unthinking glorification of political democracy. He reminds us of its empty boasts, and of its costly mistakes. But political democracy is only one form through which the democratic spirit may be expressed, and even in the political sphere we must distinguish accomplishment from ideal. Democracy, as we are

[1] First series, p. 5 seq.

concerned with it here, is an attitude toward life,
and because it is here, and here to stay, we must
study it sympathetically, trying to understand
not only what it has done but what it would
like to do. In contrasting types one must set
ideal against ideal. It is as unreasonable to
judge democracy by its failures as it would be
to judge imperialism or individualism by theirs.

How, then, shall we define democracy as a
spiritual attitude ? The democrat of whom we
are thinking is one who makes earnest with the
social aspects of personality, and really believes
that all men are members one of another. By a
personality he means a self-conscious and self-
determining being who has become what he is
through contact with others, and expresses himself best through relations to persons. He believes that every one has it in him to become
to a greater or less extent such a centre of helpful
social influence, and the test which he applies
to every form of progress is to ask what it will
contribute to the making and training of personalities.

The salient points in this definition are (1)
the conception of personality as potential in all
men, rather than as actual, still less as equally
realized ; (2) the part assigned to other persons,
not only in training each new personality for
self-expression, but in furnishing the only medium
through which adequate self-expression is possible.
Although the democrat perceives the limits
which now shut him out from other lives—limits

of knowledge, limits of taste, limits of character—he is unwilling to accept them as final. He need be under no illusion as to humanity as it is. He need have no blind faith in progress as though it were some mysterious force operating on us apart from our own will. But he must believe that it is in all men, even the worst of them, to be better than they are, and that we must help one another to become so. More than this, he must be convinced that only through this effort in his own case will he develop his own fullest life.

In accepting this definition we avoid several common errors. We do not confuse democracy with equality. By the religion of democracy we do not mean the religion of the crowd. The apotheosis of the average man has done and is doing much harm in the world, but it has nothing to do with democracy, as we have defined it. The democrat does not believe that all men are equal either in character or in attainments. He knows very well that one man is not as good as another for any purpose to which you may set him. He does not suppose that God has the same word to speak to every one or the same work for every one to do, but he is sure that God has some word to speak to every one, and some work for each person to do.[1] The equality in

[1] Walter Page was a typical democrat in the sense in which we are here using the term. His biographer says of him : " Page had a profound respect for a human being simply because he was a human being ; the mere fact that a man, woman, or child lived and breathed, had his virtues and his failings, constituted

which he believes is the equality of opportunity ; the unity after which he aspires makes room for difference.

Nor is the democracy of which we are thinking the same thing as the rule of the majority. A belief in the rule of the majority is compatible with the belief in a necessary conflict of interests between men. The rule of the majority helps to reduce the evils which result from this conflict, but it does not remove them. After their combination as before, the units who make up the majority may remain self-centred, often antagonistic. The conception of democracy here advocated, on the other hand, starts with the postulate that the individual is not an isolated unit, complete in himself. He is a member of a larger society through loyalty to which his own best interests are realized.

This accounts for the large part which belief in progress plays in the thinking of democrats. In principle there is no reason why democracy should not be as compatible with a static philosophy as imperialism or individualism. But in practice the conditions for completely realizing

in Page's imagination a tremendous fact. He could not wound such a living creature any more than he could wound a flower or a tree. Consequently he treated every human being as an important member of the universe. . . . Page said ' good morning ' to the doorman with the same deference that he showed to Sir Edward Grey, and there was not a little stenographer in the building whose joys and sorrows did not arouse in him the most friendly interest " (*Life and Letters*, vol. ii. p. 297).

the democratic ideal do not yet exist. The limitations which give point to Dean Inge's criticism of existing democracies are patent to every observer. They can be removed only through a process of education in which the capacities latent in each individual are fully developed. This requires patience and goodwill on the part of those who teach, and also provision for organized teaching on a larger scale than has yet been attempted by any existing Church or State. The democrat believes that such organization is possible, and he is committed to the attempt to create it.

Democrats differ in their estimate of the difficulties to be overcome before the democratic ideal can be realized. Some believe that democratic religion is to-day everywhere practicable if only those who are really democrats in spirit would make their conduct match their creed. Others, no less convinced, do not share the hope of a speedy victory. They see that imperialism and individualism have deep roots in human nature, and a needed part to play in human progress. They realize that for a completely democratic society a long preparatory process of education is necessary, and that in the meantime we must find some way to live with men of other types in a spirit of brotherhood. To them the immediate duty is to multiply the points of contact between men and to trust to time to do the rest. But all democrats believe that the way to know God is to understand men, and the way to understand men is to trust the best that is in them.

These principles and convictions mould the religion of the democrat. Because he thinks of God to-day as in the past as engaged in making and training persons, he expects to commune with Him best through fellowship with persons. He values his hours of solitude because they make possible visions of truth, beauty, and goodness which he can share with others. He tests institutions by their ability to fit men to co-operate in the discovery and appropriation of spiritual values on the widest possible scale.

The conception of God as a great helper, training men to be helpful, determines the character of the democrat's religion at every point. It determines the character of his worship. Since God is the Father of many children, the better he comes to know God, the more he will care for men. It determines the character of his education. He studies God's word in nature and in the Bible, but he includes in his library of revelation the " living epistles " who walk and work by his side. It determines the character of his discipline. He keeps his body under ; he rules his desires, and masters his will, but it is to make himself a more effective instrument for doing his share of the common work. Service performed in the democratic spirit becomes in the truest and fullest sense social service—work done not simply for others but with others. The

missionary motive which is the very life-breath
of democratic religion is not only a desire to give
to others, but to make givers of others.[1]

3. Democratic Religion in contrast to Imperialism and to Individualism

This analysis will make clear to us what the
democrat's religion has in common with the

[1] This conception of democratic religion, it need hardly be
said, is very different from another which has recently found
advocates in the circles of pluralistic philosophy. According
to this view, God is not simply the guide and teacher of a progressive society, but is Himself the subject of progress. He,
too, is moving toward an end He cannot foresee, and engaging
in experiments of whose outcome He is as ignorant as their
human subjects. To those who take this view of democratic
religion it seems unworthy of their dignity to own any sovereign,
even one who is divine. As human kings have yielded place
before the rising tide of democracy, so God Himself must step
down from His heavenly throne and become a comrade among
comrades. If, in His upward course, He stumble and hesitate,
it will only give His human comrades the better chance to help
Him. The true God of this type of democrat is society itself,
in its ideal aspects, and each individual as a part of the ideal
society.

It is perhaps sufficient to say of this version of democratic
religion that those who advocate it show little understanding
of the driving forces in living religion. If our analysis of the
religious experience has been even measurably correct, a God
to whom one did not look up would be a contradiction in terms.
There may be limitations for the Deity to overcome ; but what
makes Him God is man's confidence in His power to overcome
them. The God of democratic religion is in a true sense comrade,
entering by sympathy into each human life, and helping it to
its appropriate goal ; but He is a comrade who is adequate
to every changing need, and who asks of those to whom His
help is daily extended this only, that they in their turn should
become helpers of others.

other religious types which we have studied, and wherein it differs from them. Democratic religion takes its departure from the altruistic impulse in man. Democrats, to be sure, have no monopoly of altruism. Love of one's fellows is as natural to man as love of self. The imperialist feels it as well as the democrat, and even the most thoroughgoing individualist is not immune. But the democrat's altruism differs from the altruism of others both in range and in character. To them love to man is a corollary which follows from love to God, and extends only as far as God may require. To him it is an integral part of love for God, which cannot exist without it.

For one thing, the democrat's sympathy with men extends further than the sympathy of the imperialist or the individualist. The imperialist gives alms to all, but fellowship to those who are within the Church or who may eventually enter it. The individualist is drawn to those who share his own type of experience but feels repelled by others. The ideal of the democrat is a sympathy as wide as man.

Not only is the democrat interested in more people. He is interested in a different way. His fellow-feeling takes the form of a willingness to learn as well as to teach ; to receive as well as to give.

This difference in the conception of human fellowship reflects a difference in the view of the

divine purpose. The imperialist does not expect
to receive anything helpful from those who are
outside the Church because of his conviction
that in matters affecting man's salvation God
has chosen to speak only through the Church.
The individualist expects no help from men of
differing experience because he is convinced that
the message he has received is God's final word
to him. But the consistent democrat believes
that it is God's nature to impart Himself freely
to all kinds of people, and he expects messages
from God to come through uncongenial or un-
promising people, whose insight differs from
his own.

The gifted Roman Catholic, Alice Meynell, to
whom Francis Thompson owed so much, has
given us in a poem called " The Unknown God "
a moving description of the fellowship which
Catholic religion makes possible. In the celebra-
tion of the Mass, the most august of all the
sacraments, when God intervenes directly in
miracle, she finds room for human sympathy.
As she kneels, waiting her turn to go up to the
altar and to receive at the priest's hands the
body of her Lord, she is conscious of a worshipper
kneeling at her side who has just partaken of
the sacrament. She becomes vividly aware that
the Christ whom she has come to meet is even
now revealing Himself to this disciple. He is
unknown to her, but he is no stranger to her
Lord. Christ is present in his heart ; and her
spirit, crossing the barriers of ignorance and

mystery, appeals to the Christ who is blessing
her brother to bless her also.

> One of the crowd went up
> And knelt before the Paten and the Cup,
> Received the Lord, returned in peace, and prayed
> Close to my side—then in my heart I said :
>
> " O Christ, in this man's life,
> This stranger who is Thine in all his strife
> All his felicity, his good and ill,
> In the assaulted stronghold of his will ;
>
> " I do confess Thee here,
> Alive within this life ; I know Thee near
> Within this lonely conscience, closed away
> Within this brother's solitary day.
>
> " Christ in His unknown heart,
> His intellect unknown, this love, this art,
> This battle and this peace, this destiny
> That I shall never know, look upon me !
>
> " Christ in His numbered breath,
> Christ in His beating heart and in His death,
> Christ in His mystery ! From that secret place,
> And from that separate dwelling, give me grace."

Without a sympathetic understanding of this
experience we cannot do justice to the democratic
element in Roman Catholic religion. We have
called attention to the way in which through
the penitential system Rome fosters the sense
of individual responsibility. But the gift of
forgiveness offered to each penitent spirit in the
Mass is not meant for him only. The Church
offers him the opportunity of individual salvation, but also the privilege of helping to save
other souls. There is much in the practice of

If possible, the line between the true and the false is still more sharply drawn in the older Protestantism. The Christian shows his gratitude to God for salvation by means of helpfulness to all, but sympathy is reserved for fellow-disciples. The first effect of the Protestant emphasis upon individual responsibility was to narrow social sympathy. Altruism took the form of sharing with others, but not of receiving from them. Indeed, the early Protestants did not suspect that there was anything to receive. This type of religion made strong characters but narrow ones. In Geneva or in Scotland, where the Church controlled the State, a high standard of social morality was maintained,—not always by methods we should approve to-day. Little was known or cared about people of distant lands, or of other faiths. Imperialistic Rome, not individualistic Protestantism, first made world-wide missions a reality.

But Protestantism possessed one asset which was lacking in Catholicism, and that was the open Bible. The Bible has always been the great school of democratic religion, for the Bible tells us the story of religion in the making, and in its

believe that his Protestant neighbour may be saved. The Roman Catholic's acceptance of Trinitarian baptism as valid further simplifies the case, for it makes the great majority of Protestants members of the Roman Catholic Church living in schism, and relieves them of the burden of Adam's sin, of which they would otherwise be guilty. For such persons a perfect contrition, which is theoretically possible to them, would take the place of the other sacraments, of which their lack of understanding has deprived them.

pages many different types of religion find expression side by side. Our Protestant fathers were preparing the way for better things when they took the Bible as the text-book of religion, and insisted on the right of each believer to interpret it for himself. To be sure, they did not themselves realize what they were doing. They assumed that all true believers would interpret the Bible alike. Their theory made no place for the differences which did in fact emerge. Only later and under the influence of a different and a more tolerant philosophy did their successors discover that unity and variety are not necessarily inconsistent, and begin to find their way to a truly democratic religion.[1]

[1] The process, to be sure, was slower than could have been wished, and did not always lead along the lines one would have anticipated. Of the two types of individualistic religion we have distinguished, negative or legalistic religion, and positive or mystical religion, we might have expected the latter to show itself the most effective school of democracy. And in the case of the Friends this expectation has been justified. But it has not always proved so. Of the two branches of European Protestantism, Lutheranism and Calvinism, Lutheranism has, on the whole, laid most emphasis upon the mystical aspect of religion. It has concentrated attention upon a typical individual experience which it would have all who came after reproduce without change. Calvinism, on the other hand, has made much of the law of God, and points men to the Bible, as the sufficient rule of faith and practice. The difference, to be sure, is only one of emphasis, not of absolute contrast. Calvinism has had its mystics as well as Lutheranism, and Lutheran divines make place in their theology for a *locus* on the law of God. Still, the difference of emphasis is there, and it has had unforeseen consequences. It is not Lutheranism, with its mystical interpretation of justification and the sacraments, but Calvinism, with its proclamation of God's law in

Modern science gives us a conspicuous illustration of the democratic attitude in the realm of thought. In science many men are working together for a common end in the spirit of expectancy and faith. Scientists believe that the human mind is able to discover the truth. But they know that this discovery can take place only if the mind remains sensitive to every new impression. No previous presupposition must be allowed to close the door to possible alternatives. Any theory must be abandoned if new evidence is forthcoming. The independence of the reality to be known from our individual apprehension of it is one of the basic principles of science. But the scientist knows that this reality is in process of change. No previous observation, therefore, nor any number of observations can exhaust our knowledge. There will never come a time when we can say: "Now we know all there is to be known." For not only have we not yet mastered all the facts now to be observed, but new facts are constantly emerging which make it necessary to revise our previous hypotheses. And no one can tell beforehand where these facts are to be found, or what they may have to teach us.

In this attitude there is a moral as well as an intellectual element. We have referred to William James as a man who restricted his studies in religious psychology to the field of individualistic religion. But in the character of his own intellectual life he was a conspicuous illustra-

tion of the democratic spirit of science. No
scientific thinker of our time resisted more successfully the temptation to intellectual pride.
There was no form of human experience in which
he was not interested, no humblest representative
of living piety from whom he was not willing to
learn. The fact that he had not had a particular
type of experience, or that it was not congenial
to him, did not lead him to question its divine
origin or to discount its present significance.
He drew wisdom even from the pathological.
We shall find few more consistent examples of
the democratic spirit in the realm of thought.

With an apparently endless task before him,
co-operation offers the scientist the only prospect
of ultimate success. No one can see all that is
to be seen, or by himself command the conditions
of successful experiment. Therefore we must
work together. In all the lines of scientific
research an elaborate mechanism of co-operation has been established. Great laboratories
assemble multitudes of workers, each engaged
upon an individual task. But these apparently
independent studies are parts of a single whole.
They converge upon a common aim, and only
through a unification of all the different results
can a solution be reached which will command
general assent.

The single laboratory is typical of the whole
fellowship of men of science. Out of their
common search for truth in receptivity and
sympathy a spirit is often born which may

formulated a new social philosophy, the conception that reciprocal friendship, in the familiar form in which we know it in our families and in our clubs, may be extended to cover all human relationships. The founders of the first Settlements were interested in people as such, all kinds of people. Those who had fuller lives shared what they had with those whose lives had been less fortunate. They did this as learners as well as teachers. They expected to receive as well as to give. This spirit animates the whole of the newer philanthropy. Since our ideal for each individual is that he should be both giver and receiver, we are more interested in keeping people well than in curing them when they are sick; in furnishing them with work, than in supporting them when unemployed; in keeping them out of prison, than in keeping them in. If they must go to prison, then let us see to it that they are so treated while there that they will never find their way back, and let us believe that this is possible. Thomas Osborne was a conspicuous exponent of the democratic spirit when he started his society for mutual improvement among the prisoners in Sing-Sing. There is a Japanese Christian in Tokyo to-day who is running a great prison in that city on Osborne's principles, and proving that they are practicable in Japan as well as in the United States.

The democratic spirit shown by educators and social workers in their attitude toward individuals may be illustrated on a larger scale in

recent movements in industry and in politics.
Two great forces are competing for the control
of modern business—imperialism and democracy.
Socialism in its more thoroughgoing forms is
only a different name for imperialism. There
are forms of the trades union movement which
are little better. They are fighting organizations,
subordinating all to the battle against capital,
and ruthlessly suppressing individual variation
in every form. These manifestations of the
fighting spirit in labour, inevitable as they seem,
give capital its chance. They perpetuate the
class conflict in industry, and parallel in striking
ways the strife of the sects in religion. But
there is another and a better spirit abroad in
industry—a co-operative rather than a com-
petitive spirit. The exponents of this spirit are
often called socialists, and they agree with the
socialists in criticizing the present social order
as ineffective and un-Christian. But the philosophy which they hold, unlike that of the
orthodox socialists, is democratic rather than
imperialistic. They believe in conference and
experiment. They preach the doctrine of mutual
understanding. They do not believe that the
working man with his present equipment is
competent to run industry by himself, but they
believe that he may train himself to become
competent, and that even now there are phases
of industry about which he may have something
to teach his employer. The men who hold this
new conception of industry as a co-operative

enterprise wish to extend its application to society as a whole. Our present methods both of production and of distribution seem to them so stupid and wasteful, that a radical reorganization of our social and economic system is not only desirable, but practicable. But such a reorganization, if it is to be permanently beneficial, must be brought about by peaceable methods, and must command the intelligent support of those who live under it. Working men are urged, therefore, to study and to organize, but they are not told to regard men of other classes as enemies. Since all are victims of a bad social system, the co-operation of all is needed to change it.

In his remarkable book, *The Sickness of an Acquisitive Society*,[1] Professor R. H. Tawney has expressed the faith which inspires this new spirit in industry. It is the faith of democratic religion. Professor Tawney does not think that selfishness is the only power strong enough to make men work. He gives reasons for believing that the pleasure which men take in good work may be itself a sufficient motive, and, above all, the consciousness of deserving well of their fellow-men. He condemns the present industrial system as wasteful and inefficient most of all because it has not yet appealed to the nobler impulses in man or released his spiritual resources. In a word, Tawney believes that it is possible to carry the religious spirit into industry.

[1] London, 1920.

The faith that inspires Professor Tawney's book found striking political expression some years ago in a widely read pronouncement of the English Labour party.[1] In this carefully prepared document the particular measures proposed are based on an underlying conception of human relationships which assumes that co-operation rather than competition should be the law of life in society, and that peace rather than war should determine the policy of nations. While the subject-matter treated is economic and political, and the measures proposed were meant to define a party platform, the ideal expressed is independent of the changes of contemporary politics, and concerns itself with perennial realities of the spirit. We shall not be wrong if we regard it as an expression of the religious spirit in politics.

All these movements are phases of a single movement, and derive their inspiration from a common source. They are religious in that their representatives derive the ultimate motive for their activity from the common recognition of a spiritual reality superior to the individual and determinative of his ideals — truth, beauty, goodness, fellowship, as the case may be. They are democratic since they find in the common recognition of this reality, and in the common practice of the principles which follow from it, a bond of union with men and women of every

[1] "Labour and the New Social Order," a report on Reconstruction, reprinted in the *New Republic*, February 16, 1919.

race and class. For this reason a study of these
movements is an indispensable prerequisite to
an understanding of democratic religion in the
more conventional form in which it meets us in
the Churches.[1]

5. *Illustrations of Democratic Religion within the
   Churches. The New Theology. The En-
   larging Conception of Christian Missions.
   The Movement for Christian Unity*

With this background in mind we come back
to the Churches, and find that the democratic
spirit is at work in them. Even in the older
Churches, it was present, though hampered and
limited in the ways we have described. But in
the modern Church the democratic spirit is
beginning to develop its full implications, and
to create appropriate organs for its expression.
Among the most important influences which
have contributed to this result may be men-
tioned the application of scientific methods to
theology, the enlarging conception of the Church's
missionary responsibility, and the movement for
Christian unity. Before we sum up our con-

[1] Theologians of every school have insisted that the revealed
religion preserved in the Churches presupposes and comple-
ments a more inclusive natural religion. They make place,
therefore, in their text-books for the doctrines of natural, as
well as of revealed, theology. If this be true of imperialist and
sectarian theologians, how much more eager ought democratic
teachers to be to lay the widest possible foundation for the
religion of democracy in familiar human experiences often
characterized as secular.

clusions and try to estimate the value of democratic religion, let us take a final look at the
Churches under the play of these influences.

By the New Theology we do not mean to
describe any particular set of beliefs, but rather
the new attitude which results from the application of the scientific spirit to religion. The
scientific study of religion lifts us out of our
narrow environment and brings us face to face
with the fact of variation. The scientist not
only recognizes variation as a fact. He attempts
to understand the reasons for it. He enters
sympathetically into different points of view.
He tries to see things with other men's eyes, and
to measure values by their standards. He has
broken once and for all with the ideal of uniformity. He thinks of the world as not only
made but making. This conception of development which has proved so fruitful in other realms
he carries over into the field of religion. He
reads the Bible as the story of man's progressive
apprehension of the divine. In its pages he
sees many different minds reacting in many
different ways to the message of the same God.
Instead of a single revelation in the past, completed once for all, he finds God continually
revealing Himself, and he sets no limits to what
may be disclosed in the future.

One need not exaggerate the part which
science has played in preparing the way for democratic religion. There are religious teachers who
would persuade us that the only trouble with the

of personal salvation. But they have come to
see that the person to be saved is the person in
his environment, father, husband, teacher, employer, politician, labour-leader, lawyer, patriot.
You cannot change the individual without alter-
ing his standards all along the line. Men cannot
pray " Thy Kingdom come," without com-
mitting themselves to the task of doing God's
will on earth as it is done in heaven. The Social
Gospel is our attempt to define what this means
for us to-day. It is the consistent expression
of the democratic spirit in religion.

A third influence through which the democratic spirit finds expression in the Church life of
to-day is the movement for Christian unity. By
this we do not mean simply or even chiefly the
efforts that are being made to bring about organic
union, technically so called. We refer to the
movement for closer co - operation between
Christians in all its varying phases. Christian
people are becoming conscious of the fact that
the different communions are not only parts of
one all-embracing Church, but that they have
each something to contribute to its enrichment.
They are therefore eager to find appropriate
forms through which the many-sided life may
find united expression.

In their notable pronouncement on Christian
unity at the recent Lambeth Conference the
Bishops abandon once and for all the ideal of
uniformity in religion. They recognize that
there are many different channels through which

the grace of Christ may flow and that He has
in fact spoken to men by many different voices.
They do not ask the repudiation of any form of
the Spirit's ministry. They would not have any
one of these different experiences excluded from
the larger Church. They wish a Church in
which all the members of Christ's flock may feel
equally at home, however many the folds in
which they have hitherto been shepherded.
What is this, but the expression of the democratic spirit in religion ?

But Lambeth was a symptom rather than a
cause. It was only the public expression of a
spirit which has long been at work in Protestantism, and which has only failed of the recognition it deserves because of its lack of consistent
institutional expression. Considered as a form
of *organization*, the Presbyterianism of to-day is
simply the continuation and development of the
Presbyterianism of Calvin and of Knox. The
same is true of each of the other main divisions
of Protestantism. But the *attitude* which the
Presbyterian of to-day takes toward his fellow-
Christians of different communions has under-
gone a revolutionary alteration. The older
Protestantism was sectarian, in the technical
sense of that word. Each group thought that it
possessed the full truth of God and tried to
impose that truth upon its neighbours. Whether
a man was a Presbyterian or a Baptist or an
Episcopalian he insisted that he was so *jure
divino*. But to-day we grant to other Christians

and that it is capable of new and far more effective application.

But neither representation nor federation will accomplish what is asked of them if any existing form is regarded as a finality. Since democratic institutions must give expression to a growing and developing life, they cannot be rigid or unchanging. They must contain within themselves provision for self-improvement. For this a foundation must be laid in a comprehensive system of *popular education*. Boys and girls need to know more than how to read and write. Even the best possible vocational training is not enough. Our future citizens must be taught to see their special tasks as parts of a larger whole. They must be helped to realize their personal responsibility for making a success of the great co-operative experiment we call democratic society. This conviction underlies our belief in universal popular education, however far in practice we may be from realizing our ideal.

It is obvious that to provide institutions which shall be adequate to the needs of a truly democratic society all three of these principles must be applied simultaneously, and each with due regard to the operation of the others. Unfortunately this has nowhere been done. The institutions of society have nowhere been consistently shaped according to democratic ideals, but represent compromises, more or less conscious, with other types of social philosophy. The principle of representation has been most generally adopted. But it has been accompanied by no corresponding education in the principles which should govern the vote, and with the principle of federation, with a few notable exceptions, we are just beginning to experiment.

What is more important, we have not realized that in our experiments with democratic government we have begun at the wrong end. We have put political democracy first, which is the most difficult of all forms of government, while in our industry and in our religion we have left a free field for the strife of imperialism and individualism. But it is in connection with the things which lie nearest at hand, our work and our worship, that we must begin our experiments with democracy if we are to hope for success.

One reason for this failure has been the lack until recent years of a true conception of education. We have thought of education as dealing with special studies apart from and in addition to the work to be done in factory or in business. We have thought of it at most as training the individual for his own particular trade or interest. We have not conceived it as the means through which to interpret to the members of the rising generation, whatever their particular business may be, the life which as free citizens they are to live together.

What is true within each nation is true *a fortiori* of the different nations. We suffer to-day in the field of international relations because we

have as yet devised no institutions through which
the free spirit, present to a greater or less degree
in all the different nations, may find a common
vehicle of expression.

Nevertheless real progress is being made.
In industry, as we have seen, the democratic
spirit is at last working out institutions for its
expression. All the principles to which we have
referred, the principle of representation, the
principle of federation, the principle of universal
education, are being applied in modern industry
on a constantly increasing scale. A body of
experience is being acquired which is bound to
exert, indeed which is already exerting, a reflex
influence in political and in more narrowly
educational circles. From many different centres
influences are at work which need only to be
co-ordinated and guided to provide the foundation for a truly democratic organization of society.

What is going on in industry, in politics,
and in education is going on also in the Church.
In many different ways the different Christian
bodies, dissatisfied with their present divisions,
are working out forms appropriate to democratic religion. In the local community, in the
missionary and educational work of the Churches,
between the different denominations as a whole,
various forms of union are being devised. Community Churches are being formed, Federations
of Churches are being set up, nation-wide Federal
Councils are being established. Plans are being
made for extensive co-operation in the field of

religious education.[1] What the end is to be, we cannot yet foresee. But we shall fail to read the signs of the times if we do not perceive that in these new experiments the democratic Church of the future is feeling its way to a more complete and adequate self-expression.

What this Church is to be like, only the future can reveal. But it is possible even now to sketch the broad lines which the development must follow.

For one thing, it will be a Church. Whatever else the religion of democracy may be, it will be religion. Now, as in every age, the hunger of the soul is for God, and those institutions only can hope to survive which can satisfy this hunger. Worship, then, will be central in the Church of the future—the worship of the one Father by His many children.

Again, the Church of the future will be a free Church. It will have but one way of maintaining its unity, and that is through the agreement of its members in conviction and in experience. These open-minded Christians will be reverent of the past, and ready to learn all that it can teach, but chiefly for this reason, that the study of the past will make possible new creative experiences, present and future.

Above all, it will be a developing Church. It will not only leave room for wide variety in its forms of worship and methods of activity,

[1] For the details of this movement in the United States, cf. the author's work, *The Church in America*, New York, 1922.

12

but it will be constantly revising these forms
and methods in the light of new experience.
The members of this developing Church will never
regard their work as finished.   They will always
be trying new experiments.   They will be continually comparing experiences in the hope of finding
some better way.   Conscious of serving the living
God, their faces will be turned to the future;
they will set no limits to their expectation.

More than this it is not possible to say.   How
this new Church will be organized, how it will
function, will be determined by those who come
after us.   We may hazard the conjecture that
it will make much larger use than we have done
of the principle of federation.   For federation is
of all forms of government that which has faced
most completely the problem of unity in variety.
Of this we may be confident, that whatever form
the future organization of the Church may take,
it will conserve the best in the experience of the
past, and make place in the present and the future
for that free co-operative experiment which we
have seen to be the life-breath of democratic
religion.

CHAPTER VI

THE UNIFYING PRINCIPLE IN RELIGION

1. *Review of the Ground traversed. The Resulting Questions* (a) *as to Personal Responsibility,* (b) *as to Attitude toward Others*

WE have studied three typical forms of religion — imperialism, individualism, and democracy—and we have tried to find out wherein they differ.

It may be asked, How does this help us? We were led to undertake our study in the hope that we might find some principle which would not only clarify our thinking, but would help us to act more effectively. It would seem that we have simply added to our existing causes of perplexity a further divisive element.

Even if this should prove to be the fact, it will have been worth while to make the study. It is futile to try to persuade ourselves that life is simpler than it really is. If men differ in the ways we have described, it is important for us to know it. Whether we realize it or not, to one or other of these three types we belong or to

some one of the possible combinations between
them. If this be so, let us recognize the fact
and be able to give a reason for our position. It
may be that in clarifying our thinking about
our own type of religion, we shall discern more
clearly what ought to be our attitude toward
men of other types.

We began, it will be remembered, by calling
attention to the problem of variation in religion.
If religion be the all-important thing religious
people agree that it is, why should they differ
so widely as to its nature ? This fact of difference
meets us wherever we turn. Not only do the
great religions differ from one another, but they
differ within themselves. They differ in organization. They differ in belief. They differ in sentiment. And in many cases these differences are
so deep-seated and persistent as to prevent all
personal intercourse. How comes it that the
adherents of the same religion are unwilling to
meet at the same table or to worship in the same
church ?

We recalled some of the more important
historic explanations. We tested the theory
which contrasts a particular type of religion as
true with all others as false. We considered the
explanation which finds the key to the differences
of the historic religions in their contribution to
the development of religion as a whole. We
found that neither of these explanations alone
can account for all the facts. In all the historic
religions, and through all the different stages in

the development of each religion, we discovered the presence of certain persistent parallel types which we called imperialism, individualism, and democracy. By imperialism we agreed to understand a type of religion whose representatives believe that they serve God most acceptably when they submit to the control of some existing institution, the supremacy of which in the world they identify with the triumph of God's will. By individualism we agreed to understand a type of religion whose representatives despair of satisfaction through any existing institution, and find solace in immediate communion between the individual soul and God. By democracy we understood a type of religion whose representatives are convinced that they serve God best when they discover His presence in other persons, and unite with them in the progressive realization of the ideal social order which it is God's purpose to establish on earth through the free co-operation of men.

We saw that these contrasted types cannot be completely identified with any existing form of historic religion. Institutions are compromises between different points of view. Every Church includes people who belong to each of our three types. We may go further and say that no individual is perfectly consistent in his religious life. Like the larger groups to which we belong, each one of us is a living compromise, responding from time to time to differing and often inconsistent stimuli. There is something of the imperialist in each one of us, something of the individualist, something of the democrat. It is only in hours of crisis, when the choice must be made, that we learn to which competing rival our major allegiance is given.

This constant shifting of emphasis gives the study of history its fascination. As in nature new variations are constantly appearing which are the result of cross-breeding, so in man. At some of these variant types we have already glanced in passing. The religion of the sect is such a type. It owes its origin to the marriage of individualism and imperialism. The spiritual religion of the Friends is a similar variant. But the parents in this case are individualism and democracy. The Friends carry the rejection of forms to an extreme which no individualist can surpass, yet they associate it with a social passion which has made them the leaven of our modern world. Into these interesting bypaths we have not tried to enter. We have been content to point out that the three great types which we have been contrasting are persistent types, and that the recognition of their existence is essential to the understanding of the problems of present-day religion. How does this conclusion help us to understand our own religious life ? What light does it shed upon the attitude we should take toward those who differ from us ?

2. *Tradition, Intuition, and Experiment as Influences determining Personal Faith. Different Use made of these by Imperialist, Individualist, and Democrat. Place of the Creative Experience in each*

Clearly our first question concerns our own individual responsibility. What is to be our personal attitude toward the three types we have distinguished? Shall we be imperialists, individualists, or democrats, or shall we follow some one of the possible intermediate paths? Or, if we find—as in ninety-nine cases out of a hundred we shall find—that the decision has been made already, how shall we justify our choice?

On any level of life, this is a momentous matter, but for the religious man it is difficult to overestimate its importance. In religion we are dealing with the ultimate reality. The question is not simply how we shall relate ourselves to our fellow-men, but how we shall relate ourselves to God. Which road will conduct us most directly into His presence? And what shall we find when we are there?

Only experience can give us our complete answer, and this is true whatever path we take. There is a story by O. Henry called *Roads of Destiny*, in which a young traveller comes to a place where three roads meet. He must choose which of the three he will follow. When the road first chosen has been traversed, the author brings his hero back to the starting-point, and lets him take the second road, and then the third. The point of the story lies in the fact that at the end of every road he meets the same destiny.

I am not sure but that, taken as a parable of life, the end of this story is truer than its beginning. When it comes to our ultimate decisions, conscious choice plays a much smaller rôle than our text-books of morals would have us believe. For most of us the main path is determined from the start by circumstances over which we have no control. It is the little choices we make after we are on the road for which we shall be held responsible. Not what we do is the decisive thing, but how we do it. Whether a man is to be an imperialist, an individualist, or a democrat will for the most part be determined for him. This of itself will not necessarily decide his ultimate destiny. That will depend upon the spirit in which he meets his problems. It is not the path that determines the issue, but the man who travels it. Given the same consecration and sincerity, each road may lead to the Father's House.

But the roads may differ in length, and the obstacles may not be the same. To overlook this fact would be to misread our study, and to miss the lesson. It makes a difference, to myself and to others, which of these three types of man I am. It makes a difference in my relation to God, and it makes a difference in my relation to my fellow-men. When we say that our ultimate choices are determined for us, we do not mean that we should accept them blindly or without due appreciation of their significance. To live at our best we must make our own by conscious appropriation what birth, inheritance, and education have made of us. We do not choose our country, but we do decide what citizenship shall mean to us. We may not choose our religion, but we should understand it. If I am to live under the Stars and Stripes, let me know what it means to be an American. So if I am to be a member of the Christian Church, let me know what it means to be a Christian. And the same is true of each of the types of Christianity which we have described. As an imperialist or an individualist, I should know why I am such and be able to give my reasons. As a democrat, I should have a more convincing justification for my position than passing sentiment or unconscious imitation. I am not freest when I break away from the path on which my feet are moving and turn aside to follow my own caprice. I am freest when I see clearly the goal toward which my path is leading me, and follow it because it is bringing me where I wish to be.

The question why I am any one of the possible types of religious person is but one form of the more fundamental question why I am religious at all. How do we know that in religion we have real communion with God? What convinces us that our experience introduces us to objective reality and that belief in God is more than a subjective illusion—a personification of desires resulting inevitably from our unwillingness to accept our finite limitations?

The question meets us in a double form. How do we know that there is a God to speak? How do we recognize Him when He has spoken? In theory these two questions may be distinguished. In life they are inseparable. One never believes in God in general, but always in some particular God of whom one has or hopes to have experience. So far as the imperialist in religion differs from the individualist and the democrat, he differs in his conception of God. He thinks of God as having such and such a purpose and as revealing Himself in such and such a way, whereas they conceive that purpose and that revelation differently.

In determining why we believe in God, then, we are not raising a different question from the question why we are imperialists or democrats. We are only bringing out the larger implications of the inquiry. To justify my position as a democrat in religion I must be able to show that God cares for every human being, and has ways of making Himself known directly to each. To prove my case as an imperialist I must demonstrate that God's infallible revelation comes to men only through the Church.

It is not easy to put into words the reasons which do, in fact, convince us that there is a God. We do not win our ultimate convictions by argument. " They spring not from reason, but deeper inconsequent deeps." They are part of the capital we bring with us into the world. They are the premises from which all our subsequent conclusions are drawn.

How do we know that we exist ? that we love ? that we are free ? that there are other persons with whom we have intercourse ? that physical nature is independent of our thought of it, and not a mere picture that our mind paints for us ? How do we know that truth exists ? or goodness ? or beauty ? that there is such a thing as duty ? that there is such a thing as honour ? We know these things in the same way that we know that there is a God. We believe in each of these ultimate realities because we needs must. We find such belief implied in the life we live day by day. And the same is true of our faith in God. We believe in God, because unless there is a reality corresponding to our thought of God, our world would lack coherence and significance, and the things we do from hour to hour would lose their meaning and their sanction. Philosophers have clothed this elementary fact in learned language. They have called it the ontological argument. But it comes to this at last, that what is essential to the continuance of my spiritual life I must believe to exist if I am to continue to live in the spirit. To the religious man God is such a necessity.

" Why do you believe in God ? " I once asked a clever woman of my acquaintance. " You would not understand me if I were to tell you," she answered. " So far as I know myself, I have three reasons for believing in God. The light in some people's eyes ; the sense of honour ; and the joy which follows complete surrender to a cause that is greater than self." I do not know that any theologian has ever put the real reasons for believing in God more convincingly. *We believe in God because there are experiences in life at once so arresting and so significant that apart from God it is psychologically impossible for us to account for them.*

Easier to answer, but still difficult enough, is the question how we recognize God when He speaks. Three possibilities are open : 1. We may believe that God has spoken because of what others tell us. 2. We may know that He has spoken because we ourselves have heard Him speak. 3. We may be confirmed in our belief that He has spoken because we have obeyed Him, and have found our belief verified by experience. We may call these three ways of justifying belief in divine revelation : (1) the method of tradition ; (2) the method of intuition ; (3) the method of experiment. Imperialists, individualists, and democrats use all three of these methods, but they use them in different ways and arrive at different results.

Many people find in what others tell them a sufficient justification for religious belief. They grow up in a world in which there is faith, and they accept the faith they find. It never occurs to them to do anything else. They may look for guidance to the Church, or to the Bible, or to the tenets of their own little sect or community. But whether it is to be Church, or Bible, or creed will be settled for them by others. Whatever their neighbours accept as revelation they accept. They are not even aware of the existence of an alternative.

If a time comes when they can no longer evade the question Why? they may still find in tradition a sufficient basis for conviction. They may say, " It is not reasonable to suppose that God should expect me to answer this momentous question alone. There must be some authority which will relieve me of the responsibility. When I have found it, I will commit my conscience to its keeping, and be sure that I am doing God's will."

By this road they may be led back to the conclusion with which they started, only now their conclusion will have deeper and more personal significance. Now they believe in authority, because it is morally and intellectually satisfying for them to do so. In Newman we see an acute intellect accepting the principle of tradition *con amore* and finding the peace which he seeks. It is the typical attitude of the imperialist — the point at which he parts company with the individualist and the democrat.

But the question still remains, Where is the true tradition to be found ? and here personal responsibility cannot be evaded. Before I can trust my Church, I must find a Church to trust. There are various ways in which this can be done. I may convince myself by logical arguments that the true revelation is only to be found in such and such a place, because there alone are to be found the marks by which revelation is recognized. Much of historic theology consists in the effort to define what these marks are, and to show that as a matter of fact they are present in the institution or the book to which the character of revelation is assigned. Sometimes these marks are found in evidences of intelligence in nature, as in the teleological and cosmological arguments ; sometimes they are found in the exceptional and inexplicable events we call miracles. More often in a combination of both. But in each case the effort is to demonstrate that in the particular concrete fact or facts with which revelation is identified there are present qualities which the spirit cannot but recognize as evidencing God's presence.

But the argument forces us a step further. How can I tell that this rather than that is the handiwork of God ? Whether my attention is directed to the orderly processes of nature or to the exceptional events we call miracles, how do I know that they point me to God rather than to blind force, or impersonal law ? Even granting that the occurrence of miracle can be established, why is there anything divine in miracle ? Why not see in miracle mere chance, the proof that we have come to a place where reason breaks down, and chaos begins ?

There is only one way to meet this issue. We must press back of logic to intuition. If I am to infer God's presence from His handiwork, I must know beforehand what kind of a being God is, and what qualities are likely to reveal Him. You cannot take out of your conclusion more than you have put into your premise. If I am to recognize God when He speaks, it can only be because there is some capacity in me which fits me to do so.

All truly religious people are convinced that they possess such a capacity. They not only believe that there is a God ; they are confident that He can speak to them, and that they can recognize His voice. The name we give to this inner response to the divine communication is intuition.[1] It is the one final and convincing proof of revelation.

We commonly associate the use of intuition in religion with persons of mystical temperament. But it cannot be so narrowly confined.[2] All three of the types we have been studying in these lectures make large use of intuition. The im-

[1] In choosing the word " intuition " to describe man's immediate response to what is apprehended as divine, I am not using the word in any technical psychological sense, but as a convenient term to describe any form of experience of reality which carries its own conviction with it.

[2] On the mystical element in belief in miracle, cf. my essay, " The Permanent Significance of Miracle for Religion," *Harvard Theological Review*, July 1915, p. 314 seq.

perialist believes that the visible Church is the
channel of God's revelation, because there is
something in him which this belief satisfies.
The individualist knows that God has saved his
soul, because he has an inner peace which cannot
be explained in any other way. The democrat,
too, finds in intuition the basis of his assurance.
He is confident that God is speaking to others as
well as to himself, because he has heard what
they have to tell him about God, and his own spirit
answers to what they say.

Intuition, then, is common to all forms of
vital religion.[1] But the use which is made of
intuition differs widely. The mystic is sure that
he has heard God speaking. Yet he cannot tell
you what God has said. No human language
can describe an ineffable experience. Each of
us must entertain the divine visitant for himself.
Other Christians can give you a more definite
answer. They can tell you where they have
recognized God's voice—in the Church ; in the
Bible ; in the life-story of some friend, as the case
may be. They can recall what the voice has
said to them, now a word of comfort, now of

[1] All our ultimate convictions rest at last upon intuition.
It is common to art and to science. In the last analysis, the
quest of truth appeals to some mystical sense in man, that joy
in the immanent divine which is the spring of the great religions.
Poincaré gives utterance to this insight in his book on *Science
and Method* (Eng. trans., London, 1914), when he interprets the
joy of the mathematician in his most recondite calculations as a
form of the quest of beauty. It is harmony in which he takes
delight, the highest and the most perfect which the mind can
apprehend.

warning, now of enlightenment, now of forgiveness, now of inspiration.   They can point you to
the place where you too may hear God for your-
self, and they can tell you what you may expect
to hear.

But what if the voices disagree ?   In other
phases of our experience, when faced with a
conflict of testimony, we have recourse to experiment. We follow the working of each of the
possible alternatives, to ascertain which most
completely accounts for the facts.

We may do the same in religion. Religion,
as we have seen, is not simply an individual
experience but an historic process. We believe
that God is the ruler of society as well as the
Father of individuals ; that Jesus is not only
personal Saviour but the founder of the Kingdom
of God. If this be so, we ought to find indica-
tions of this fact in the world about us. Our
faith should not rest simply upon the satisfaction of our private need. It should find
confirmation in God's working in history.
Here, as in a laboratory, we may use other
men's experience to supplement our own, and
test the hypothesis of religion by co-operative
experiment.[1]

At this point the individualist parts company
with the imperialist and the democrat. He
would confine his experiment with God to what
his own soul can compass, whereas they would

[1] Cf. W. Adams Brown, *The Essence of Christianity*, New
York, 1902, pp. 295–309.

13

enlarge the field of experiment to take in other men. The imperialist would have you submit to the Church, whereas the democrat would have you trust the best that is in each man. Both extend the test beyond the individual ; but the kind of experiment to which imperialist and democrat invite differs widely. The conditions which the imperialist lays down would make impossible any other test than his own, whereas the democrat would keep the field open for the trial of every possible experiment. His type of religion needs no such limitation as the imperialist requires. On the contrary, free variation is of its essence. To confine experiment within any limits but those which the religious life itself sets would rule out the possibilities in which the democrat finds his most inspiring hope.

Thus it appears that the representatives of each of our three types use all three of the great historic methods of justifying faith in God— the method of tradition, the method of intuition, the method of experiment. The difference between them is rather one of emphasis and of proportion. The imperialist gives greater weight to tradition than the individualist or the democrat ; the individualist lays most stress upon intuition ; the democrat gives widest range to experiment. Yet each recognizes that the other methods have their place, and uses them within limits.

But whatever weight the representatives of these three types of religion may give to each of the different elements in their approach to God, they agree in this, that the final test of religious faith for the individual must be its liberating effect upon the spirit. In the type of religion to which each yields allegiance, he is conscious of access to some new spring of wisdom, of power, and of joy. The imperialist may find God in the Church, the individualist in his own soul, the democrat in fellowship with kindred spirits. In finding God, each finds life more abundant. To each, religion is a creative experience. For each this creative experience carries with it its own evidence as to the nature of religion and the purpose of God.[1]

3. *The Problem of Relationship. Attitudes excluded. Need of a Unifying Principle* (a) *for Self-Criticism,* (b) *for Social Verification. The Creative Experience as such a Principle*

From the question of personal responsibility we pass to the question of social relationships. When we have chosen for ourselves, what follows for our attitude to those who have chosen differently ? What shall we think of them ? How ought we to feel toward them ? Above all, how far can we work with them ?

[1] On the Creative Experience, cf. W. Adams Brown, *The Creative Experience an Intimation of Immortality* (London, 1923). We use the term here in a comprehensive sense to describe any form of experience which releases fresh energies, and makes its possessor conscious of greater power, larger insight, and deeper satisfaction.

Some possibilities are ruled out from the start. If what we have been saying is true, it will no longer be possible for us to ignore these other types of religious experience. The men and women who share them must henceforth enter into our world, and the problem of our personal religious life will become in part the problem how we are to relate ourselves to them.

Nor can we any longer be content with a purely negative attitude toward the views we do not share. We cannot say that other men are wholly wrong and that we are wholly right. Still less can we comfort ourselves with the thought that different religious types represent merely temporary phases, which, having played their part, will pass away. If our conclusions have been correct, three great types at least are recurrent, each appealing to something fundamental in human nature, each winning its converts from the new generation, as the old is passing away. Individuals here and there may change ; the types will remain.

One further possibility is excluded. We cannot maintain an attitude of indifference, as if it made no difference to which type a man belonged. The issues between imperialism and democracy are real issues. They are even momentous issues. It makes a difference, not only for the individual, but for society which is to control. Our appreciation of other types of religion must not make us less loyal to our own. The unity after which we aspire must not only be consistent with our existing differences, but must make possible intelligent discrimination between them.

But is such unity possible ? Can religion furnish any platform on which we can all alike conscientiously stand, while at the same time it gives us a standard by which we may sympathetically appraise the differences which divide us ?

In the past such a standard has been found in a common acceptance of historic revelation. Men might differ in their understanding of what God's revelation meant, and where it was to be found. But they were agreed that God had revealed Himself in history, and that the record of that revelation had been preserved. By appealing each in his own way to this authoritative standard they believed themselves able to justify their own position against their opponents. Such an appeal was entirely natural and reasonable. If God is to reveal Himself to persons, it must be in history ; for it is in history that the individual contacts take place through which personalities are formed. The sublimest utterances we possess, those which present us with truth of most permanent and universal value, have come to us out of the experience of individuals who have preceded us, and in a setting which we can date. The story of religion in its main outlines is the story of its creative spirits. The great man, the great book, the great work of art—through these the successive generations find their best selves and are trained to approach God for themselves.

It is natural, then, that men should turn for confirmation of their present beliefs and practices to the standards which have maintained themselves through the centuries—the Bible, the creeds and traditions of the Church, the Christ to whom Bible and Church alike witness. The difficulty with this method as hitherto practised has been that the use made of these standards has been too arbitrary. They have been interpreted in a manner foreign to their genius, and used for purposes for which they were not intended. Each has brought his own presuppositions to his reading of history and found there the confirmation he sought. Is the appeal to the Bible? " *Hic liber est in quo quaerit sua dogmata quisque.*" Is tradition to be the final authority? Abelard draws his deadly parallel in the " *Sic et non.*" Thus what was designed to unite, has proved in fact divisive. A unifying principle, to be really effective, cannot stop with the formal standard to which men appeal. It must determine the use they make of it. We must know not only what men profess to believe, but why they believe it and what consequences follow from their believing.

Such a principle of comparison is given us in the creative experience. We have seen that this experience is common to all three types of religion. Imperialists, individualists, and democrats will tell you that their choice has made possible for them a fuller life. It has

liberated unsuspected energies ; it has induced
enduring satisfactions. The apparent negations
of historic religion really prove the rule. Sacrifice
is not end but means. Renunciation is required
in order to make possible a more complete
affirmation. One denies oneself in order to enjoy
a fuller life.

But if this principle of testing religion by its
fruits in life be recognized as valid by the advocates of each of the contrasted types in their
estimate of their own kind of religion, why may
it not furnish us with the test we need for judging
between them ? Our answer to the question how
far each is socially desirable will be determined
by our judgment as to how far each is able to
enlarge and enrich the life of those who embrace it
*without limiting the possibility of a similar enlarge-
ment and enrichment of life in other persons.*
Religion must rely for its ultimate justification
not on what it forbids, but on what it brings to
pass. The unifying principle in religion is its
life-giving power.

Yet though the test is the same in the larger
as in the narrower experiment, the manner of
applying it will be different. We are not thinking here simply of individual satisfaction, important and significant as that is. We wish to
know what is the capacity of a type of religion
to *reproduce itself in a succession of experiences
and to create institutions which shall develop to
the utmost the personalities living under them.*
This is a test which requires us to take account

of other men's experience as well as of our own, and to measure the effects of the type we champion by studying its remoter as well as its more immediate consequences.

Such an inquiry is a wholesome corrective to hasty judgment. It is easy for any one of us to be content with a congenial type of religion without inquiring what would be its effect if universally adopted. But we should not stop here. The democrat must ask himself how far his democratic religion can provide the satisfactions which others find in imperialism or in individualism. The imperialist must test himself by his ability to meet the needs of the individualist and the democrat. The individualist must come to terms with all those who have found their satisfaction in institutional religion.

It is true that the answer which any individual can give to this question will be limited by his own experience. Any test which is to be really adequate must be based upon an induction of all the evidence available. And this requires cooperative study on a far more extensive scale than we have hitherto found possible. But at least we can affirm that the attempt to measure the value of a religion by its power to enlarge and to enrich human life would give us a principle on which men of very different presuppositions could unite, and so would make possible the social verification without which any individual decision, however conscientiously arrived at, must be at best provisional.

4. *The Creative Experience as a Principle of Unity within Christianity*

We may illustrate the way in which emphasis upon the creative aspect of religion brings unity into a field where differences seem most irreducible, in connection with a question which has caused much controversy in the past — the question, namely, what is distinctive in historical Christianity ?

Most of those who will read this book call themselves Christians. However much we may differ in the details of our faith, we stand in the same historic tradition. We read the same Bible. We acknowledge the same Master. We pray the same prayer. In contrast to men of other faiths, we believe that in the history through which we trace our spiritual ancestry, God has given us a message of far-reaching and indeed of universal significance. It is from Jesus, not from Gautama or from Mohammed, that we hope most for the world's salvation. Yet when we try to point out just what the distinctive message of Christianity is, we find ourselves dividing in the ways already described. Imperialist, individualist, and democrat—each defines Christianity in his own way. The imperialist sees in Jesus the founder of the Church, the incarnate Word whose divine human life is perpetuated in the Sacraments, the world ruler who has committed to Peter and his successors the administration of His authority and the mediation of His grace.

The individualist sees in Him the heroic spirit who dared to break with the Church of His day, in order to find His own way to God. The democrat sees in Him the friend of man as man, the discoverer of unsuspected capacities for good in the outcast and the despised, the founder of the better social order we call the Kingdom of God. For each, Christ is central. To each, loyalty to Christ is the distinctive Christian virtue. Yet loyalty is so conceived by each as to separate him from, rather than to unite him with, his fellow-Christians.

Underlying this procedure is a common presupposition—that Christianity is a single changeless type from which there can be no departure. Much learning has been expended in the attempt to define this type, and many different methods have been used to discover it ; [1] but common to all is the assumption that Christianity is something uniform and changeless—a dogma, an institution, a particular type of conduct or experience. No one of the methods hitherto used makes

[1] In their search for the distinctive in Christianity, scholars have used different methods. Sometimes the origin of the new religion has been determining, and we are told that we should eliminate from our definition of Christianity everything which is the result of later influence. Sometimes the clue has been sought at the end rather than in the beginning, and Christianity is identified with what it is coming to be. Or still again, a definition may be reached by abstracting from each of the different parallel forms whatever is distinctive, and finding the essence of the religion in what remains.

When put to the test, no one of these methods proves adequate. The method of origins fails us ; for it is only in the

room for the freedom and flexibility with which history presents us, and so their advocates are forced to deny the legitimacy of types which differ from their own, or to explain them away.

It is evident that we must approach our problem from a different angle. We are dealing with something that is alive, and we must treat it accordingly. We cannot abstract any part of a many-sided life, and treat it as the whole. All parts of Christian history are necessary to the understanding of any part of it—beginning, ending, and all that lies between. Yet this does not mean that all are equally important, or equally informing. We wish to discover the creative element in Christianity, the thing that has made institutions but which no institution can confine, which has formulated itself in creeds but which no creeds can express, the inner genius or spirit which is perpetually reproducing itself and giving rise to new creative activity in others. This original but at the same time permanent and creative element in Christianity, most Christians

light of the later history that we can tell what part of primitive Christianity was really novel and creative. The method of outcome fails us, for we are not yet far enough on in the history of our religion to know what the final issue will be. Least of all can we hope from the method of averages. To attempt a cross-section of all the different forms of historic Christianity is to miss that which is original in each. It leaves us with a colourless abstraction, which, whatever else it may be, is not the living religion in which men have heard God speaking to them face to face. Cf. W. Adams Brown, *The Essence of Christianity: A Study in the History of Definition*, New York, 1902.

would agree, must be found in the personality
of its founder.

When we say that Jesus is the distinctive
element in the Christian religion, we do not mean
that Christianity is simply the imitation of Jesus.
Christianity is much more than this. " Forward
with Christ " expresses its genius better than
" Back to Jesus." We mean that through all
the centuries Jesus has been the source of new
creative experience in others. Contact with Him
has helped men to see God for themselves. In
following Him they have learned to do things
for themselves. When Jesus said to His disciples
that they were not only to reproduce His works,
but were to do greater things still, He gave fittest
expression to the spirit of His religion.

This new and creative aspect of Jesus' influence has been expressed in the Church's faith
in the living Christ. In this faith Christians have
voiced their conviction that through the lips of
this brother man, God is speaking to them, and
in his life they see God's character and purpose
revealed. But the method in which the confession has been made is itself a striking example
of the dual influence of history.

Rightly interpreted, the doctrine of the living
Christ is a doctrine of freedom. It is the refusal
to confine God's witness to the past. Much
as Jesus meant to the first disciples, He was to
mean more to those who came after Him. For
each new generation He has had some new
message, some fresh inspiration. When the shell

of the past has pressed hardest and the deadening influence of habit has robbed the older forms of their fresh and original meaning, contact with the figure of Jesus as depicted in the Gospels, has opened new windows into heaven, and set new life-currents coursing through men's veins. To Catholic, to Protestant, to men of other religions, to men of no faith at all, Jesus has proved Himself the Word of God—the point of contact between the human and the divine.

When, however, this vital aspect of Jesus' personality has been allowed to fall into the background, the doctrine of Christ's Deity has had precisely the opposite effect. The shell has pressed so hard that it has stifled the life it was meant to protect. Instead of teaching that Jesus has set each of us free to seek God for himself, theologians have explained the doctrine of Christ's Deity as meaning that it is sinful to let our thought of Jesus differ from the thoughts of other men before us. Instead of assuring us that God is like Jesus, and therefore we can go to Him freely and boldly, they have told us that since Jesus is God, He cannot be the friendly human figure the Gospels make Him. When one studies the history of dogma, and compares what it is to what it might have been, one is led to repeat the cry of Mary at the sepulchre, " They have taken away my Lord, and I know not where they have laid Him."

Yet while men's theories about Jesus have divided them, their experience of His influence

has united them. The life they owe to Him
brings them closer to one another. The imperialism that takes Jesus for Master creates a finer
type of character than other imperialisms. Christian mystics owe a profounder experience to their
contact with Jesus. Democratic Christianity includes unifying elements which are not present
in other democracies. As we learn to know the
different types of Christians better, we are confirmed in our conclusion that no one type of
religion can include all the truth or do full justice
to the beautiful and the good. Yet we are equally
convinced that there is something in the Christian
religion which transcends these differences and
makes it possible for men who have felt the life-
giving influence of God's Spirit to respect and
to work with one another. We may still differ
in much and feel bound to defend our differences,
but we shall differ as fellow-disciples and as
fellow-worshippers.

What is true of the central figure of Christianity is true of the agencies by which His
influence has been mediated. Considered as
objective standards, rules of faith and conduct,
the Church and the Bible have proved divisive.
Considered as creative influences, helps to a
richer and a fuller life, they have proved unifying.
We find saints in all the Churches, and we are
helped to understand the Bible by what it has
meant to St. Francis and Pascal, as well as to
Calvin and Wesley.

5. *The Creative Experience as a Test in the Conflict of Religions*

If it is difficult to tell what is distinctive in a single religion, how much more difficult is it to find the unifying principle in religion as a whole ? A study of the creative element in religion may suggest a helpful point of approach.

If we review the methods hitherto used in missionary apologetic we find ourselves involved in many difficulties. These difficulties are in part due to our own differences—our failure to agree as to just what Christianity is, and what is the test by which it must be judged. But they are accentuated by the attitude of the people to whom we come. They are not people without religion. With negligible exceptions, they have traditions and institutions of their own. They are as conscious as we of possessing a divine revelation ; differing as widely as ourselves in the way they interpret it. All the different varieties of religion which we have been studying in these pages meet us in all the greater religions. It is not simply that we bring a Christianity which is divided. We face a Hinduism, a Buddhism, a Mohammedanism which is divided, and in part by the same issues. If we come to them bringing our own type of Christianity—Presbyterian, Episcopalian, Baptist, they point to other Christians who do not share our views, and ask why one type of Christianity should be preferred. If we point out this or that feature of our religion

as justifying its claim to be regarded as God's
final revelation, they present a similar claim on
behalf of their own. The moral excellence of the
Biblical teaching will be admitted by the Con-
fucianist, but he will remind you that China has
lived under the ethics of Confucius for two
thousand years. If we lay stress on the supernatural features of our religion, and emphasize the
Christian doctrines of the incarnation and the
atonement, the Buddhist can point to his own
supernaturalism, and for the single incarnation
in Jesus Christ, offers us a continual succession
of Buddhas. If we take our stand on the
authority of the Bible as a divine and infallible
book, the Mohammedan has the Koran, which
claims an infallibility even greater. If in our
desire to discredit the religion of our opponents,
we apply the process of criticism to the standards
of their religion, they remind us that critics have
been applying similar processes to the study of
Christianity ; and we shall be fortunate if the
scepticism we succeed in evoking in their minds
can be arrested at the point we have marked
for it.

Yet all the time another debate has been going
on, and another test is being applied, all the
more significant because largely unnoticed. It
is the test of the creative experience. Each
religion has brought its contribution of insight
and of enlightenment, of inspiration and of hope,
and men have responded in the ways most natural
to them. They have taken what was helpful,

and let the rest go by. They have adopted, rejected, modified, reconstructed, according to the urge of the life within. The test of the relative strength of the different religions has been the extent of their ability to release the creative energies of men. That religion will conquer the world which *deserves* to conquer, and the proof of its desert will be the test to which Jesus appealed—its ability to produce more abundant life.

It is encouraging to find that this test is finding theoretical recognition in recent missionary literature. What men *ought to think* of religion is less emphasized than what religion is actually *able to do* for men. What is it in Christianity which appeals to the Moslem as a matter of fact? what repels him? What, on the other hand, is there in Mohammedanism to which the Christian responds? [1] A debate carried on on these lines will uncover the real issues, and with its disclosure of differences will reveal unsuspected unities. Doctrines that are cut off from their roots in life are as much a travesty of the convictions of living religion, as the dried plants that are preserved in our *herbaria*, of the flowers that bloom in our gardens, or the fossils that we discover in the rocks, of the trees under whose shade we take refuge from the sun. When we touch the vital forces within each of the great religions, we have a clue to the true relation of

[1] Cf. the suggestive series of articles on this subject in the *International Review of Missions*.

14

the different religions to one another. In the measure that this test is conscientiously accepted and systematically applied, we shall be in a position to make an intelligent estimate of the place actually held by our own religion in the conflict of religions.

Some years ago a theological teacher was asked by one of his class whether the unique value we Christians attach to the Bible was not simply the result of our upbringing; whether, if we had been born in India or in Japan, we should not have felt the same of the sacred books of Hinduism or of Buddhism? A young Japanese who was a member of the class asked the privilege of replying. He said, " The case described was my own. I was converted to Christianity by reading a copy of the Bible. I knew nothing of Christ but what I found in this book, but when I read the Gospels they spoke directly to my soul; and I said to myself, ' This is God's word to me.' I had no difficulty with the Christianity of the Bible. It was only after I met Christians that my troubles began."

What is true of the Christian book is true of all the other agencies through which Christianity makes its appeal. The test by which Christianity must finally be judged is the test of life. Most of all is this true of the great personality whom all Christians claim in common. We shall persuade men that Jesus is God's supreme Word to men, not by insisting that they shall accept our definitions about Him, however important and satisfying they may seem to us, but by introducing them to Him, and letting Him speak to them in their own language, as He has spoken to us in ours.

6. *Consequences for our Study.   Creative Elements in Imperialism and in Individualism.   The Place of the Creative Experience in Democratic Religion.   Democracy as the Religion of Hope.*

The test which the Japanese student applied to the Bible is the test by which the competing types of Christianity must themselves be judged. They must stand or fall by their power to enlarge and enrich life. So far as any one of the three types we have been studying helps men to a richer and a fuller life, it is good and ought to be encouraged ; so far as it narrows and impoverishes it is bad and ought to be condemned. But, if the test is to be significant, it must be applied by each of us consistently to his own type of religion, as well as to those which are unsympathetic. We must not compare our ideal with others' practice ; but test ideal by ideal, and performance by performance.

Let us suppose that one is a democrat in his religion. As he looks back over his life he sees that all his experience has been leading him inevitably to this conclusion. To be a Christian to him means to be a democrat. This view of religion corresponds most completely to what he finds in the Gospels. It sheds the brightest light upon the dark pages of history. It answers

the deepest needs of his own soul. He thinks
of Jesus as of a friend who is continually revealing the possibility of new friendships—a builder
who has set his hand to a task which cannot be
completed unless all of us do our share. But
while this is true for him, he realizes that it is
not true for others. To them Jesus brings a
different message and seems to point along a
different path. He dares not deny that the
Word which they hear is God's Word. He is
not an imperialist. But he recognizes that the
imperialist who accepts Jesus as his Master will
be a different and a better man from one who does
not. He is not an individualist. But he is
sure that the individual who makes Jesus the
companion of his solitude will find something for
which Christless souls search in vain.

How far ought this recognition to go ? Where
is the point where appreciation ought to stop
and criticism begin ? How far can we feel that
the work which our fellow-Christians of other
types are doing promotes the values which to us
are inseparable from the Christian religion ? How
far must we see in that work a menace which we
are bound to resist ? I answer : so far as that
work is constructive and not destructive ; positive, not negative ; creative, not simply the vain
attempt to preserve the memory of a life which
has passed away.

Tested by this principle each of the three
types we have been studying has much to say for
itself. Within limits each can be justified by its

work. Criticism begins when—in the effort to control other lives—a method which has proved useful and legitimate in its place is used to limit the creative spirit in its present effort to find new forms of expression.

Imperialistic religion, when studied in its great historic examples, is seen to be one of the constructive forces in human history. It has been a builder of institutions, and a teacher of the men who have lived under them. It has come to men living in narrowness and isolation, and presented them with an ideal which has lifted them above themselves. In times of depression and inertia, it has preserved the records of a past which without its machinery of conservation might have perished for ever. It has given men world-wide tasks. It has made possible international fellowship. It has provided discipline and happiness for those who were too weak to stand alone. And so far as it still does these things, it is good, and those who give their lives to its service may be welcomed by men of other types as comrades and fellow-workers.

But when imperialistic religion goes farther and claims all life for its field ; when it denies to the men of to-day the initiative and freedom to which it owes its own origin ; when it would confine God within a single channel and overlooks His presence in men of other types—then imperialistic religion becomes a menace ; and the protest of individualist and of democrat is justified.

So we may admit that individualistic religion has much to say for itself. Tested by our principle of the creative experience, it has vastly enlarged and enriched human life. This is true not only of the individual men and women who, in order to fulfil their personal destiny, have broken away from the crowd to live their life in privacy. It is true no less of the larger company who have become the beneficiaries of their insight. All God's greatest words to men have been spoken first to some one man ; and Jesus— the friend of man—found that He could not fulfil His social mission unless He replenished His soul through solitary hours alone with His Father.

So far as it makes possible the larger life, then, individualistic religion is good, and place must be made for it in our religious philosophy. But when the individualist makes his own life the standard for all others, he ceases to be constructive, and becomes a hampering influence. He impoverishes himself, for he loses the new word which God might speak to him through his neighbour. He impoverishes others ; for by so much as he reduces his own stature, he limits his power to do for them.

This insight explains and justifies the democratic experiment. Democracy is the attempt to break free from the limits which imperialist and individualist have set to the possibilities of new experience. The democrat is not willing to confine God's Spirit within a single channel. He gladly admits that men may find God in other than the democratic way. But he is convinced that his method makes possible the largest number of contacts, and so the most enlightening experience. Much as we may have received from God in the past, the democrat expects that the future will be richer still. To discover and to appropriate the as-yet-unrealized good is the task of the religion of democracy.

But democrats, too, need to be tested by their own principle. They, too, stand or fall by their ability to enlarge and to enrich life. It is not enough to criticize. We must construct, and this not simply within the limits which are congenial to us—among the circles of our family, our community, our personal friends—but in the great world which imperialism claims for its field, and among backward and undisciplined peoples.

It is to be feared that not all democrats have faced the seriousness of this test. Much so-called democracy is parlour democracy. Its advocates have not visualized the real task, or measured the obstacles to be overcome before the democratic ideal can be realized. Imperialistic religion asks, at most, loyalty to an institution. The field of the individualist's conflict is his own soul. But democratic religion tests progress by what goes on in all other lives. What infinite patience, what more than human sympathy is required if we are really to care for the undeveloped personalities all about us, and to find in their progress and final victory our highest reward.

And when the sympathy extends beyond one's own country and race and takes in man as man, the test becomes harder still.

On faith as well as on works democratic religion makes heavy demands. To win a living faith is never easy. We have seen how the sense of individual weakness has driven men to seek security in the Church, and how the protest of conscience against the Church has forced earnest spirits back upon themselves. But the democrat in religion must find God everywhere, and point to common men and women as the most conclusive evidence of His presence. His faith requires him to believe that God is making out of humanity as we see it to-day—stumbling, blundering, short-sighted, narrow-minded men and women—the Christian commonwealth of his dreams. Imperialism demands the surrender of freedom. Individualism must abandon the hope of unity. Democratic religion, could it be realized, would conserve both.

There are men and women who believe that this realization is possible, more to-day than there have ever been. And wherever this belief is living and active it has worked beneficent transformations. We have seen this faith at work in our science, in our education, in our philanthropy, in our industry. It enlarges the range of friendship. It is the inspiration of modern missions. From it springs much that is best in the life of the Church. But there are wide areas of our life—even of our religious life—which have thus far been inaccessible to the democratic appeal. Is this resistance permanently to continue, or will democratic religion reveal a constructive power adequate to the tasks which imperialism alone has thus far been able to discharge ? That is for the future to decide. It is enough if those of us who hold the democratic faith do our part in the present to make that better future possible.

In what were perhaps his last printed words about democracy, that great democrat, Viscount Bryce, sums up his conclusions as follows :

" Hope, often disappointed but always renewed, is the anchor by which the ship that carries democracy will ride out this latest storm, as it has ridden out many storms before. There is an Eastern story of a King with an uncertain temper who desired his astrologer to discover from the stars when his death would come. The astrologer, having cast his horoscope, replied that he could not find the date, but had ascertained only this, that the King's death would follow immediately on his own. So it may be said that democracy will never perish till after hope has expired." [1]

It is because we believe in this better future and are trying to realize it that we call ourselves Christians. Of all existing religions, Christianity has most to give the democrat. Mohammed commits us to imperialistic religion. The emphasis of the Buddha is predominantly on the individual. Only the religion of Jesus has room

[1] *Modern Democracies*, London, 1922, vol. ii. p. 670.

enough for democracy. It has something for
the individual—for each the inspiration and
assurance he most needs. It has something for
all of us together—a fellowship of the spirit more
inclusive than any other known to man. It has
faith and comradeship. It has the forward look.
Christianity is not yet the religion of democracy.
But of all existing religions, it has the best fighting
chance to become so.

INDEX